CW00854111

Simple Steps to Building Successful Cosmetic Practices

By

Yasmin Khan

Bright Pen

A Bright Pen Book
Visit us online at www.authorsonline.co.uk

Book design and layout by Lush©
Visit us online at www.lushdesign.biz

ISBN 978- 07552-1132-6

Authors OnLine Ltd
19 The Cinques
Gamlingay, Sandy
Bedfordshire SG19 3NU
England

This book is also available in e-book format,
details of which are available at www.authorsonline.co.uk

About the Author

Yasmin Khan

Yasmin Khan is the founder of K-T Group Inc., an international management consulting, training and resource firm specializing in Medical Cosmetic Training and Strategic Management for rapid growth. Ms. Khan is the former International Sales Manager for Inamed (Facial Aesthetic Division) and Collagen Corporation (US). She has combined her 14 years of global marketing and sales experience in medical aesthetics to form a unique group of companies dedicated to teaching clinic owners the art of running successful and profitable aesthetic practices.

In addition to her consulting work, Ms. Khan is sought after by the media as an expert on Medical Aesthetic Marketing and Medical Aesthetic Procedure Training. She is the consultant to many of UK's top clinics including the prestigious Beauty Society and Rejuvadent.

Ms. Khan is the founder of K-T Training, United Kingdom's first training institute for Non-Surgical Medicine. K-T Training provides comprehensive procedure training in non-surgical medicine. This division of K-T Group also provides business training to medical professionals which includes leadership training, customer service training, telephone sales and practice management training for practice owners.

Ms. Khan is the also the founder of BAC (Beauty Advice Centre-www.beautyadvicecentre.co.uk), the only dot com company committed to promoting independent clinicians to the web market enabling its clients to compete against the large national clinics. To receive a copy of her newsletter, please contact K-T Training at www.kttraining.co.uk.

Key

 = Re Cap

 = Warning

 = Key Point

Thank You

There could never be a Simple Steps to Building Successful Cosmetic Practices book without the help of many individuals, especially those physicians who have allowed me to experiment with new innovations and promotional ideas within their practices throughout my career.

I would like to thank Dr. Peter Ilori for his contribution and invaluable advice on a number of issues.

I would like to thank my mom and dad for being who they are and for encouraging me to go after my dreams.

Most importantly, I want to thank my husband, Adrian Tucker, for his continued support in everything that I do.

This book was written for a global audience. I chose to write in US English. However, references to procedures' prices are in Sterling. Physicians using different currencies can substitute their local currency into the calculations. The choice of currency does not influence the outcome of the subject discussed.

Content

Training – Consulting – Medical Marketing

K – T Training Services

- Muscle relaxant training
- Dermal filler training
- Chemical peel training (training on a range of peels)
- Advance muscle relaxant and dermal filler training
- Radiesse training
- Mesotherapy training
- Dental block training
- Diet and nutrition for anti-ageing and beauty training
- Make up artistry
- Customer service and telephone sales training
- Developing and managing your medical aesthetic business
- Cosmetic dermatology and skin management

K – T Solution Services

- Change management consulting services for small, medium, and large medical and dentistry practices
- Business development consulting services for dentistry and medical practices
- Strategic management consulting services for medium to large medical and dentistry practices
- Business coaching for practice owners and practice managers
- Software integration consulting services

Beauty Advice Centre Services

- Internet marketing for independent clinicians
- Web design services
- Web script development

K – T Medical Marketing Services

- Operation manual for dental and cosmetic practices
- Simple Steps to Building Successful Cosmetic Practices book sale
- Non-Surgical training manual for administrative staff
- Software solutions for small practices
- Internal marketing presentation for open house seminars and in-house marketing
- Dentistry practice manual
- Brochure Development
- Medical and Dental Aesthetic Posters

If you would like more information on K-T Group and the services we provide, please visit our website at:

www.kttraining .co.uk or www.k-tsolutions.com

Among the things you can do on these sites are:

- Subscribe to our electronic newsletter
- Take a mini audit to see how customer focused your practice is
- Check out our business solutions
- Check out our practical training programs

Introduction

Today's medical cosmetic practice engages in a challenging and complex environment. Almost infinite numbers of medical professionals of all specialties are entering the aesthetic market, and yet there are only limited numbers of potential aesthetic clients available. In traditional medical practices, patients are forced, due to need, to use insured services whether or not they liked the practice or the staff, and are willing to put up with whatever treatment they receive.

Today's aesthetic clients do not need medical services in the same way. Aesthetic clients do not clinically need cosmetic procedures – they desire aesthetic treatments because they believe that the results will enhance their appearance resulting in a better quality of life. Clients also have unlimited choices of where to find the treatments they desire. Technically, aesthetic patients are truly consumers of cosmetic procedures, and as such medical professionals may refer to cosmetic clients as patients. Nonetheless, practice owners and their staff should never forget that aesthetic patients are clients and as clients they continually evaluate the service they receive from every industry, including cosmetic practices, and will not hesitate to switch if the service they receive does not meet their expectations.

Purposely, throughout this book I refer to patients as clients and consumers. A client will behave and respond differently to the clinician's advice relative to a patient. A patient will take any advice the clinician offers and will not challenge the clinician. Clients are usually more sceptical of the clinician's advice. Clients need to like and trust the clinician before any recommendation is accepted and acted upon. The relationship between a medical professional and the client is different, and it is the medical professional/consultant who has to over-deliver on service to win and keep the client's business. Clearly this type of relationship is different from the traditional patient/ doctor/ nurse/dentist relationship.

As greater number of doctors of all specialties, venture capitalists, dentists, and independent nurses compete for the limited private customer base, new and existing cosmetic practices will ultimately fail without sufficient business training. Moreover, the treatments provided by large or small practices are not unique and there are little differentiation among suppliers of medical aesthetic procedures. Hence, potential aesthetic clients have no way of differentiating one clinic from another except by reviewing procedure pricing. It is dangerous to compete against other practices on price alone. This strategy will continually erode practice growth and profitability and the result will be declining profit and longer hours at the office.

Even so, how do companies such as BMW, Mac Cosmetics, and Primark, who are in equally competitive industries, become industry leaders and claim an expanding market share?

These companies focus on customer performance as the real product. What these companies have in common — beyond their awe-inspiring success — is their dedication to their customers' results. Like scores of today's like-minded market leaders around the world, they are on the cutting edge of the most important strategic transformation of the decade: the shift to 'customer intimacy'. These companies have given up the old mindset 'us versus them' to embrace a single common insight. The largest source of growth, advantage, and profit resides in the design and development of 'customer focus relationship' (Fred Wiersema, p5).

Customer focus relationship does not mean customer satisfaction, or customer choice, or reacting to your customers every whim - focus companies discover how to provide complete solution for their customer's needs. In doing so, they become indispensable partners with their customers - in essence these companies are building an emotional bond between themselves and the customer.

Let me give you an example of what I mean by emotional bond. I have visited my local coffee shop almost three times a week for the last three years — yet no one knows my name, the type of coffee I like or even bother to acknowledge me when I enter the building. This company obviously does not understand the concept of customer relationship. If it did, it would choose employees who are friendly, happy and willing to serve. This coffee shop scenario exists since there is little competition in its market place. I can assure you that as soon as another café opens up which offer a smidgen of service, I as well as others will quickly move.

Most customers return to their favourite restaurants, coffee shops and most other establishments on account of the added value provided through an emotional connection. Customers prefer to feel good about any transaction they make. If a medical practice can inject this concept of creating an emotional bond with its customer into its strategy, and train its employees to serve its' customers, the result will be highly motivated and loyal customers who will sustain the practice's long term growth objectives.

Customer centric businesses stand out and customers are loyal to businesses that provide superior service. Marks and Spencer is a prime example of a troubled business that does not seem to know its customer's needs while Primark's annual profit is a true reflection of a business that does know its customers' needs. This strategy of knowing your customers' needs and designing services and products to satisfy these needs is essential for long term success in aesthetic medicine. Return clients and referrals are what make a practice successful. Without a strong relationship and a committed customer, you are peddling commodities.

This concept of developing an emotional bond with your aesthetic clients is referred to as RELATIONSHIP MARKETING. In aesthetic medicine, relationship marketing is a necessity for the long-term growth of any aesthetic practice.

The medical industry attitude towards marketing have changed dramatically since 1994 when I began to work in aesthetic medicine. However, in certain parts of the world medical professionals still view the concept of marketing as unethical. Marketing involves many skills ranging from planning, people management, financial forecasting, promotion and advertising, market segmentation, and a lot more which will be discussed in this book. The essence of relationship marketing is to identify the needs of your customers and develop products and services to meet those needs.

Since most medical practices do not create products or services, the challenge of the medical marketer is to home in on the needs and desires of their market segments and design services which will appeal to the identified target markets. Clearly, there is nothing unethical about trying to identify the needs of clients and designing services and treatments to satisfy those needs. Therefore, employing a relationship marketing strategy for your practice is the most ethical and progressive approach to doing business in today's competitive aesthetic market.

Developing a relationship marketing strategy for any business takes time and expertise by the marketing executive. Since there are few medical marketing experts in the industry, it is my intention in writing this book to provide practice owners and their management team with a relationship strategy that is effective in attracting new clients and keeping clients loyal to your practice. Like all strategies, execution is what will determine the success of the strategy. The execution of the activities and the timeline is up to you. If the activities are executed effectively, I will guarantee improvements in: staff's attitude toward customers, customer retention, higher annual profit, and higher equity valuation of the business. If you do not have the time to execute the activities discussed in this book, you can purchase our Business in Box software which works hand in hand with this book. The Business in a Box software package is segmented into five categories similar to the book and provides you with a turn - key business program.

If you choose to hire a marketing consultant, it is important that you identify the consultant's expertise - are they skilled enough to assist in executing the recommendations discussed in this book? If the marketing consultant chooses to provide advertising solutions only, I recommend that you look for a true expert or contact K-T Group at www.info@ kttraining. co. uk for recommendations on selecting your marketing consultant.

The intention of this book is to take the complex subject of relationship marketing and strategic planning and simplify it for the medical aesthetic market. The book was developed so that a practice owner need not employ all the business principles discussed here at one time to see results. Each section discusses certain relevant relationship marketing and strategic business concepts and makes recommendations on integrating these strategies into the practice. It is my intention that this book will be used as a reference manual for you and your staff for years to come. Well, at least until the next edition!

For simplicity, I have segmented all aspects of the practice's activities into five broad categories:

- Procedure selection and technical training
- Client relationship management
- Staff development
- Internal operations
- Internal and external promotions

The contribution of each category is equally important. However, if forced to choose, I believe that procedure selection and technical training is the priority for small practice owners (where the owner is the only employee of the company). For larger practices, staff development is the priority. Staff development is essential to build a cohesive team which will drive the business to achieve its core objectives. Like the coffee shop example, it is your staff's ability to create an emotional bond with the customers that will keep them coming back and using more of the business's services and products.

Chapter 1

Procedures

In my experience most clinicians believe that they have to provide unbridled variety of treatments to remain competitive in the market. This situation exists because aesthetic clients are proactive in asking for what they want or believe they want. Furthermore, most clinicians feel that they have to provide unlimited choices to satisfy the client's needs.

This is the incorrect approach since most new medical aesthetic treatments are not new innovations but duplication of existing science based products already on the market. Providing clients with unlimited choices is inefficient and shows that the practice does not understand its client's needs. This strategy of offering everything is an indication that the clinic owner or his/her marketing expert has not identified their market segments and is choosing to offer everything in the hopes that customers will find something that interest them.

This strategy rarely works and the clinic will lose out in the long run because a clinician can rarely develop expertise with every product or treatments that exists in the market.

It is best to develop expertise in a few core treatments rather than try to be a master of all treatments. Loyalty between you and your client will rarely develop if the treatment result is mediocre. Remember, cosmetic clients gather information from the Internet and through popular health and beauty magazines. I have spent a lot of time working with journalists to promote different products and quite frequently the published articles do not provide the level of information needed to help clients make an accurate assessment of their needs.

The same goes for the Internet. Free advice offered on internet cosmetic sites focuses on how to assess the practice and clinician's credentials, since there are a lot of unskilled clinicians in the market.

For instance, there are some sites that even advise clients to request specific amounts of units of botulinum toxin to be injected when choosing muscle relaxant treatments. The problem with this advice is that it is misleading and ignores the fundamental issue. Every client is different and one recommendation might be correct for some and completely incorrect for others. To develop an intimate relationship with your cosmetic client, it is fundamental that you help your clients to define their concerns, and it is up to you as an expert to recommend the best and safest treatment options available to the client.

You are providing poor service to your clients if you react passively to their request without making an effort to discuss their overall needs and set realistic expectations for the clients. Of course you should provide a broad range of solutions, but your decision on what to offer should not be influenced by the most recent article on a new product or popular Internet sites.

Ultimately, your practice will be more successful if you focus your efforts on providing excellent treatment outcomes on fewer procedures. I will discuss what these procedures are in the latter part of this chapter.

1.1 The Importance of using statistics for procedure selection

This section is long because it is necessary to understand the importance of using statistics before decisions on products and procedure integration are made.

Before you introduce any procedure or product into your practice you should ask yourself, "will my customer like this treatment and will they be willing to pay for it"? If the answer is no ,do not introduce the treatment into your practice. If you do not know your target market and their needs, this section is intended to teach you the basics of market segmentation.

I joined Collagen Corporation in 1994 and in those days I dealt predominantly with plastic surgeons, since they were already providing cosmetic treatments (surgical). In those days, it was not uncommon for surgeons to refuse to offer non-invasive treatments in their practices since these services were perceived as low revenue generating, inferior to surgical procedures, and most importantly — the procedures were not permanent.

A decade later, things have certainly changed. Non-surgical treatments are, and have been for some time, the largest growing segment of the medical aesthetic industry. If surgeons had looked at statistical trends, they would have seen this coming and made the necessary changes within their practices to capture this market. Those who did are now miles ahead of the game. I emphasized my experience with surgeons to highlight a similar mistake which is being made today. While everyone will agree that non-surgical medicine is definitely the growth industry, clinicians still make decisions on procedure offering without referring to statistics. Instead, medical professionals choose to attend conferences where they are inundated with manufacturers claiming their product is the must have to compete effectively in the market place.

Unlike the past, where medical professionals could make costly financial mistakes and survive, this is impossible today. The market is tremendously competitive and medical professionals cannot afford to make poor financial decisions. The most effective means of managing financial risks and increasing opportunities for long term success is to look at past statistics to determine the core procedures that are driving the market globally.

There are hundreds of treatments in the European medical aesthetic market but many are not evidence based and rarely produce the results claimed by the manufacturer. Recommendations by sales representatives, colleagues, and most importantly opinion leaders who are compensated by large manufacturers, should be evaluated against solid quantitative data.

Some of you may have familiarity with Isolagen. This US based company closed down its UK franchise in 2007. The company decision to close down its UK operation was probably perpetuated by the large number of complaints from former clients and their patients. The US based company targeted dentists and physicians by employing a pull strategy. The company engaged in extensive promotion to the public resulting in large customer demand for the treatment. However, there was insufficient evidence of treatment predictability and efficacy. Medical Professionals were attracted to the product because of the high profitability of the treatment and the manufacturer's marketing support. However, the product did not produce the results the manufacturer claimed and at £4,000/treatment, clients wanted justification as to why they were misled and why alternative treatments which could have provided superior treatment outcomes were not discussed.

The outcome has been financially damaging to clinics that provided a large amount of Isolagen's treatments. Had clinicians who provided Isolagen treatment evaluated the company's claims against the US statistics, they would have been less likely to introduce this treatment into their practice. Poor treatment selection will ultimately result in patient dissatisfaction and damage to the business's reputation.

To demonstrate the importance of statistics in developing your procedure mix and to segment your market, I am using the American Society of Plastic Surgeons' statistical data for a number of reasons:

- The results of the survey are based on a 95 percent confidence level with maximum error range of plus or minus 3.0 percent

- Since 1992, the American Society of Plastic Surgeons (ASPS) has been the sole source of cosmetic and reconstructive plastic surgery statistical trends in the U.S and Europe

- The five year trend report is a universal and comprehensive estimate of cosmetic plastic surgery procedures and non-surgical procedures performed by ASPS member surgeons as well as other physicians most likely to perform plastic surgery procedures and non-surgical procedures

- It has been observed that the American trend in aesthetic medicine is the most accurate forecast of what will occur in Europe and the rest of the world. The time lag is approximately three to five years.

Before I begin to review the statistical data, I want to introduce a few marketing concepts that will contribute to your understanding and appreciation of this section of the book.

Market Segmentation

The concept of market segmentation involves dividing your mass market (local area) into tiny segments and developing customized services and products for each segment. Most marketing driven companies are very skilled in dividing their mass markets and providing tailor made products for their segments. More importantly, the communication messages to these segments are clear and targeted.

Let's take BMW for example. The different models of cars are designed around different target markets. The 100 series is designed around the youth market who can enjoy the prestige of the BMW brand but who cannot yet afford the higher priced products. Rather than lose this market segment to other less expensive car manufacturers, BMW selected to create a less expensive product for this market segment. As this market segment matures, its needs will change and so will its income. There is high probability that most of the BMW 100 series customers will stay with the brand, and upgrade to more expensive BMW brands as they age or become wealthier.

BMW is very skilled in customer retention which explains why the company is highly profitable and commands premium pricing for its cars. In aesthetic medicine, medical marketers do not adapt any segmentation strategy and the communication message to the aesthetic market is vague, imprecise, and untargeted. For example, the medical aesthetic market consists of many smaller segments. These segments can be broken down by age groups as follows: (ages 18 or less, 19-29 age group, 30-39 age group, 40-55 age group, 55+ age group, male group and female group).

Each group has different needs, and they respond to different advertising messages. Therefore, an advertisement which consists of a clinic's list of treatments will hardly command any response since the advertisement is not communicating to any specific market segment. In the latter section of this chapter, the difference between the segments will become clear.

Why Segment Your Market?

There are several important reasons why an aesthetic practice should segment its market.

Better Matching of Clients Needs

Clients' needs differ. Creating separate offers for each segment makes sense and provides clients with better solutions. For example, the 19-29 age group have needs that are different from the 30-39 age groups. Before attempting any promotional campaign, you must identify the target group you want to attract, determine the group's needs, and customize the promotional message to the specific market.

Enhance Profit

Clients have different disposable income. For example, a 20 year-old client usually has less disposable income than a 40 year-old professional. They are, therefore, different in how sensitive they are to price. By segmenting markets, practices can raise average prices and subsequently enhance profits. This concept will become clear in later sections of the book.

Better Opportunity for Growth

Market segmentation can build sales. For example, clients can be encouraged to "trade-up" after being introduced to a particular lower-priced treatment. Chemical peels (Alpha Hydroxy Acids) for instance, are popular procedures in all the segments; therefore, an effective promotional strategy might be to offer a reduced price on (AHA) chemical peel treatments to attract a large number of individuals into your practice. Once clients are in the practice, you may use an internal strategy to move clients up to higher price procedures or TCA peels which generates more profit for the practice. Of course, the recommended higher price procedure must be appropriate and beneficial for the client.

Retain More Clients

Clients' circumstances change, for example, they grow older, change jobs or get promoted, and change their buying patterns. By marketing procedures that appeal to clients at different stages of their lives (life cycle), a practice can retain clients who might otherwise switch to competing procedures.

Target Marketing Communications

Businesses need to deliver their marketing message to a relevant client audience. If the target market is too broad, there is a strong risk that (1) the key clients are missed and (2) the cost of communication to clients becomes too high/unprofitable. By segmenting markets, the target client can be reached more often and at a lower cost.

1.2 How to use statistics to segment your market and create focused product offering

The objective of this section of the book is to review the statistical data and segment the total aesthetic market into smaller groups. Once you have identified your key market segments, you will be able to identify the top five procedures in each segment and the growth procedures in each segment. This information is useful in developing your promotional campaigns and introducing new procedures into the practice. We will discuss how to use the outcome of the analysis in your promotional and new product launch initiatives.

To determine your key market segment, you may wish to search Google for local demographic information by typing in (local demographic north London eg...). The analysis will identify the market segments by income, age, gender, buying habits and lifestyle choices. The statistics will provide you with invaluable information on your market segments. The information in this book will identify popular treatments by age group and gender. The review of the two statistics is enough for you to identify your target market's needs, lifestyle choices, disposable income and where to find them.

Target Marketing Communications

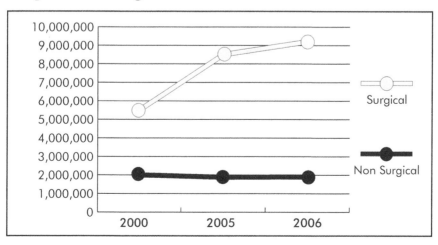

Surgical and Non – Surgical Market Trends 2000-2006

As indicated by the graph, surgical procedures as a whole have remained flat since 2000. The growth of the non-surgical market from prior year is only 7% in comparison to a growth of 43 % from 2002 to 2003. It is important to note that the high growth rate of the aesthetic industry from 2000 to 2005 contributed to the growth of most non-surgical practices. If the growth of the non-surgical industry continues its downward trend, surgical and non-surgical practices will find it difficult to maintain prior year's revenue without an aggressive marketing strategy. Taking market share away from competitive practices without a detailed and thoroughly thought out plan is difficult and expensive to do

While surgical procedures have remained flat over the past five years, there are some procedures in the surgical arena that contribute a large amount of revenue to any surgical practice and these procedures are indicated on the next page. Note that while buttocks lifts, upper arm lifts, lower body lifts, and thigh lifts contributed only a small percentage to the overall total surgical procedures, these procedures are growing in popularity and may become a major contributor to any surgical practice. In future editions, I will highlight new trends and discuss new market opportunities.

Cosmetic Procedure Trends (American Society of Plastic Surgeons)

Cosmetic Procedures – Surgical	2005	2006	% change 2005 vs. 2006
Breast augmentation (Augmentation mammaplasty)	291,350	329,396	13%
Breast implant removals (Augmentation patients only)	24,694	27,451	11%
Breast lift (Mastopexy)	92,740	103,788	12%
Breast reduction in men (Gyneconmastia)	16,275	19,881	22%
Buttock Implants	542	639	18%
Buttock Lift	5,193	3,710	-29%
Cheek implant (Malar augmentation)	9,326	8,803	-6%
Chin augmentation (Mentoplasty)	15,161	14,649	-3%
Dermabrasion	69,359	69,300	0%
Ear Surgery (Otoplasty)	27,993	30,137	8%
Eyelid Surgery (Blepharoplasty)	230,697	233,200	1%
Facelift (Rhytidectomy)	108,955	104,055	-4
Forehead Lift	55,518	52,525	-5%
Hair transplantation	47,462	27,865	-41%
Lip augmentation (other than injectable materials)	25,878	25,626	-1%
Liposuction	323,605	302,789	-6%
Lower body lift	8,696	10,323	19%
Nose reshaping (Rhinoplasty)	298,413	307,258	3%
Thigh lift	9,533	12,295	29%
Tummy tuck (Abdominoplasty)	134,746	146,240	9%
Upper arm lift	11,873	14,886	25%
Vaginal Rejuvenation	793	1,030	30%
TOTAL COSMETIC SURGICAL PROCEDURES	**1,813, 542**	**1,852,012**	**2%**
Cosmetic Procedures - minimal-invasive			
Botox® injection	3,839,387	4,090,517	7%
Cellulite treatment	43,296	33,614	-22%
Chemical peel	1,033,581	1,063,423	3%
Laser hair removal	782,732	887,039	13%
Laser skin resurfacing	271,418	262,926	-3%
Laser treatment of leg veins	155,235	144,626	-7%
Microdermabrasion	837,711	816,774	-2%
Sclerotherapy	589,768	607,067	3%
Soft tissue fillers			
Calcium hydroxylapatile (formerly Radiance)	66,182	78,849	19%
Collagen	220,632	267,339	21%
Fat	48,960	52,904	8%
Hyaluronic acid (Hylaform, Restylane)	489,554	778,285	59%
Polylactic acid (Sculptra)	46,732	54,912	18%
TOTAL COSMETIC MINIMAL-INVASIVE PROCEDURES	**8,425,188**	**9,138,275**	**8%**
TOTAL COSMETIC PROCEDURES	**10,238,730**	**10,990,287**	**7%**

2006 Cosmetic procedures

2006 top five surgical procedures
Breast augmentation
Nose reshaping
Liposuction
Eyelid surgery
Tummy tuck

2006 top five non-surgical procedures
Botox®
Chemical peels
Laser hair removal
Microdermabrasion
Dermal filler

2006 surgical procedures with highest growth
Tummy Tuck
Lower Body Lift
Upper Arm Lift
Thigh Lift

2006 non-surgical procedures with highest growth
Laser Hair Removal
Hyaluronic acid -(Restylane/Juvederm)
Radiesse™
Sculptra®
Collagen

The number of Botox® injections reported for 2006 is the number of anatomic sites injected

The top five surgical procedures listed above have remained in the top five spots since 2000. Breast Augmentation in the United States seems to be the leading surgical procedure with nose reshaping and liposuction following close by. Similarly, the Mintel Report (UK Statistics) indicates the same trend in the United Kingdom. Surgical growth procedures such as thigh lift, lower body lift and upper arm lift seem to fluctuate in popularity year after year indicating no real trend. These procedures are unique enough to attract media attention. Presently, the volume of request for these procedures is extremely low even in America. It is not beneficial for UK surgeons to invest in specialist training to include these procedures into their present surgical portfolio since it is unlikely that surgeons will ever recoup their financial investments.

The top non surgical procedures have stayed in the top five positions since 1997. Except for laser hair removal, the four top non-surgical procedures are essential skills sets needed for facial enhancement which explains why these treatments have global appeal. Radiesse™ treatment is new to the US market and its performance is low relative to Restylane treatments, but I believe its popularity will grow over time. This product can be used to add volume to large areas such as the cheeks and jaw-line and the results are longer lasting and more cost-effective for the client. In time, cosmetic clinician will learn that they need to use multiple types of volumisers to enhance the face.

Market Share of Non-Surgical vs. Surgical Procedures

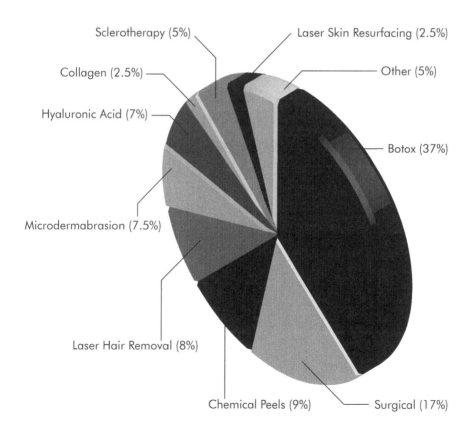

Sclerotherapy (5%) · Laser Skin Resurfacing (2.5%) · Collagen (2.5%) · Other (5%) · Hyaluronic Acid (7%) · Botox (37%) · Microdermabrasion (7.5%) · Laser Hair Removal (8%) · Chemical Peels (9%) · Surgical (17%)

In the last decade, the growing movement reflects that among the aesthetic population, only one in five clients will opt for surgery over non-surgical options. Since non-surgical and surgical clients are not mutually exclusive, it makes sense for most surgical practices to incorporate non-surgical procedures as part of the service. Non-surgical patients will generate greater amounts of revenue to the practice over the long term. It is estimated that one in two non-surgical patients will eventually elect to have some surgical procedure over their lifetime. It is best that when these patients elect to have surgery, they choose a surgical practice to do so. Furthermore, surgeons do not have to spend a penny to attract these individuals into their practices.

The same logic applies to private dentistry. Non-surgical procedures can be introduced into the dentistry portfolio to increase practice revenue and to attract new patients into the practice. Like the plastic surgery scenario, non-surgical patients will over their lifetime elect to enhance their smile, and it is best they choose your practice to do so.

"Opportunity is a haughty goddess who wastes no time with those who are unprepared". George Clason

Male Market (American Society of Plastic Surgeons)

Cosmetic Procedures – Surgical	Patients 2006 Male	% of total Male	% change 2006 vs 2005
Breast augmentation (Augmentation mammaplasty)	0	0	0%
Breast implant removals (Augmentation patients only)	0	0	0%
Breast lift (Mastopexy)	0	0	0%
Breast reduction in men (Gyneconmastia)	19,881	100%	22%
Buttock Lift	365	10%	-8%
Cheek implant (Malar augmentation)	2,875	33%	-19%
Chin augmentation (Mentoplasty)	9,304	64%	6%
Dermabrasion	8,691	13%	7%
Ear Surgery (Otoplasty)	11,063	37%	-3%
Eyelid Surgery (Blepharoplasty)	37,238	16%	13%
Facelift (Rhytidectomy)	9,256	9%	-13%
Forehead Lift	6,420	12%	-14%
Hair transplantation	20,473	73%	-48%
Lip augmentation (other than injectable materials)	1,035	4%	-20%
Liposuction	35,020	12%	-2%
Lower body lift	967	9%	-19%
Nose reshaping (Rhinoplasty)	84,570	28%	-15%
Pectoral Implants	409	100%	99%
Thigh lift	616	5%	39%
Tummy tuck (Abdominoplasty)	6,085	4%	4%
Upper arm lift	356	2%	-24%
TOTAL COSMETIC SURGICAL PROCEDURES	**255,636**	**14%**	**-10%**
Cosmetic Procedures - minimal-invasive			
Botox® injection	284,304	7%	-9%
Cellulite treatment	4,370	13%	-22%
Chemical peel	98,295	9%	-9%
Laser hair removal	172,968	19%	0%
Laser skin resurfacing	32,064	12%	-16%
Laser treatment of leg veins	19,002	13%	-29%
Microdermabrasion	182,399	22%	-9%
Sclerotherapy	7,013	1%	19%
Soft tissue fillers			
Calcium hydroxylapatile (Radiance)	5,158	7%	2%
Collagen	9,829	4%	-19%
Fat	3,719	7%	2%
Hyaluronic acid (Hylaform, Restylane)	24,664	3%	85%
Polylactic acid (Sculptra)	7,897	14%	66%
TOTAL COSMETIC MINIMAL-INVASIVE PROCEDURES	**851,412**	**9%**	**-7%**
TOTAL COSMETIC PROCEDURES	**1,107,048**	**10%**	**-7%**

2006 Cosmetic procedures - Male

2006 top five surgical procedures
Nose reshaping
Eyelid surgery
Liposuction
Hair Transplantation
Breast reduction in men

2006 top five non-surgical procedures
Botox® injections
Microdermabrasion
Laser Hair Removal
Chemical Peels
Hyaluronic Acid Fillers

2006 surgical procedures with highest growth
Breast reduction in men
Eyelid surgery
Pectoral implants

2006 non- surgical procedures with highest growth
Hyaluronic Acid Fillers
Sculptra® Treatment
Sclerotherapy

The male market segment contributed only 14% to the 2006 surgical total with a 10% decline from the previous year. Since 2000, there is a steady decline in male surgical procedures. Twenty eight percent of all nose-reshaping procedures were to the male segment. Liposuction, eyelid surgery and facelifts are also popular procedures among the male segment. However, the growth remains stagnant. It might be useful for surgeons to target the male market for these procedures but not at the expense of the female market since the female market is the true consumer of plastic surgery procedures. The male non-surgical segment contributed 9% to the 2006 total of non-surgical procedures with a 7% decline from the previous year. The growth of the male non-surgical market from 2002 vs. 2003 was a staggering 53%. However, since 2003, the growth of male non-surgical procedures in the US market has remained flat.

Muscle Relaxant treatment is obviously the most popular procedure for this segment. However, the combined total of Chemical Peels and Microdermabrasion treatments is very close to Muscle Relaxant total. This fact is an indication that men are concerned about their skin. The popularity of Microdermabrasion treatments for the male market is mainly due to the fact that the medical market has reacted slowly to this market segment's needs and the salon industry moved in first by introducing facials, laser hair removal and Microdemabrasion treatmentstomales. Itmighthelpifthemedicalaestheticmarketusesmale pictures in targeted advertisement to males, and if we better understood their needs.

 ## How to use this information

If you are planning to target the male market, it is best not to use the same advertisement you used for your female market since male aesthetics needs are somewhat different from female aesthetic needs. If you plan to target the male segment via the internet, you need a dedicated male section for your website. The appropriate term used today is metro sexual males. This term refers to males who are concerned about their overall appearance. There are many of them so a dedicated section on your website and a dedicated male brochure will reap dividends for your practice.

The statistics indicate a strong preference for skin treatments and Muscle Relaxant treatments. I recommend that your communication message to this target group focuses on skin improvement treatments, Muscle Relaxant treatments, and Laser Hair Removal treatments. When the target group is in front of you, you can recommend other services such as fillers and face volumisers. You should advise the individual on home care routine and recommend a maintenance skin program.

Female Market (American Society of Plastic Surgeons)

Cosmetic Procedures – Surgical	Patients-2006	% of total	% change
Breast augmentation (Augmentation mammaplasty)	329,396	100%	13%
Breast implant removals (Augmentation patients only)	27,451	100%	11%
Breast lift (Mastopexy)	103,788	100%	12%
Breast reduction in men (Gyneconmastia)	0	0%	
Buttock Lift	3,345	90%%	-30%
Cheek implant (Malar augmentation)	5,928	67%	3%
Chin augmentation (Mentoplasty)	5,345	36%	-16%
Dermabrasion	60,609	87%	-1%
Ear Surgery (Otoplasty)	19,074	63%	15%
Eyelid Surgery (Blepharoplasty)	195,962	84%	-1%
Facelift (Rhytidectomy)	94,799	91%	-4%
Forehead Lift	46,105	88%	-4%
Hair transplantation	7,392	27%	-10%
Lip augmentation (other than injectable materials)	24,591	96%	-0%
Liposuction	267,769	88%	-7%
Lower body lift	9,356	91%	25%
Nose reshaping (Rhinoplasty)	222,688	72%	-12%
Thigh lift	11,679	95%	28%
Tummy tuck (Abdominoplasty)	140,155	96%	9%
Upper arm lift			
TOTAL COSMETIC SURGICAL PROCEDURES	**1,596,376**	**86%**	**4%**
Cosmetic Procedures - minimal-invasive			
Botox® injection	3,806,213	93%	8%
Cellulite treatment	29,244	87%	-22%
Chemical peel	965,128	91%	4%
Laser hair removal	714,341	81%	17%
Laser skin resurfacing	230,862	88%	-1%
Laser treatment of leg veins	125,624	87%	-2%
Microdermabrasion	634,375	78%	0%
Sclerotherapy	600,054	99%	3%
Soft tissue fillers			
Calcium hydroxylapatile (Radiance)	73,691	93%	21%
Collagen	257,510	96%	24%
Fat	49,185	93%	9%
Hyaluronic acid (Hylaform, Restylane)	753,621	97%	58%
Polylactic acid (Sculptra)	47,015	86%	12%
TOTAL COSMETIC MINIMAL-INVASIVE PROCEDURES	**8,286,863**	**91%**	**10%**
TOTAL COSMETIC PROCEDRES	**9,883,239**	**90%**	**9%**

2006 Cosmetic procedures - Female

2006 top five surgical procedures
Breast augmentation
Liposuction
Nose reshaping
Eyelid surgery
Tummy tucks

2006 top five non-surgical procedures
Botox® injections
Chemical peels
Microdermabrasion
Hyaluronic Acid —Restylane
Sclerotherapy and Laser
Hair Removal

2006 surgical procedures with highest growth
Thigh lifts
Thread lifts
Lower body lifts
Upper Arm lifts

2006 non- surgical procedures with highest growth
Hyaluronic Acid (Restylane)
Radiesse™
Collagen

Approximately, 86% of all surgical procedures in 2006 were to the female market. Since 2000, there is a steady but low growth in female surgical procedures while the male figures continue to decline. Growth procedures (thigh lifts, upper arm lifts and lower body lifts) provide very little to the 2006 total but currently show strong growth over the last 4 years.

The non-surgical market only grew by 9 percent in comparison to a 40% increase in 2003 vs. 2004. Only Muscle Relaxants, Sclerotherapy, Laser Hair Removal, and Chemical Peel procedures show positive growth for 2006. Microdermabrasion has remained flat for the last two years. Notice! A larger percentage of females prefer chemical peels to microdermabrasions. It is the opposite for the male market.

This trend exists since females are turning to medical practices for their anti-ageing needs and chemical peels vs. microdermabrasion treatments are promoted more heavily in medical practices.

New physicians looking forward to entering this market, it is best to start off with the growth procedures, which luckily do not require any capital investment. If you want to include microdermabrasion treatments or laser hair removal treatments into your procedure portfolio, it is best to lease equipment in the short-term. Laser hair removal and microdermabrasion treatments are popular procedures, but these procedures can be administered by aestheticians, therefore the market is much more competitive. Before you invest in expensive capital equipment, you should evaluate the competitiveness of the market and your ability to recoup your investment in a reasonable amount of time. Do not take the spoken word of the manufacturer that you will recover your investment. In my experience, it has been very difficult to recover the capital cost of lasers and in many situations the profit generated from treatments like Muscle Relaxants and Dermal Fillers have to make up for the loss generated by expensive capital equipment.

"One does not have to provide elaborate treatments in order to achieve superior treatment outcome". Yasmin Khan

Male vs. Female Procedures at a Glance

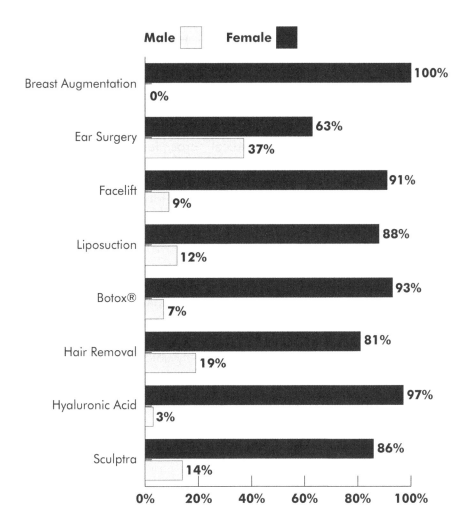

Ref: page 27 and page 30
(ASPS) 2006

If you are starting out in aesthetic medicine and plan to target both genders, it is best not to offer laser hair removal in the initial stage. The capital investment is large, and you will require Health Care Commission approval for the practice which is expensive, and in my experience, the clinic rarely recovers the capital outlay. Also, laser hair removal treatment operates in a very competitive environment since you will be competing with the beauty salon industry as well as the medical industry. Concentrate on medical procedures which require minimal capital investments such as Chemical Peels, Skin Care, Radiesse, Mesotherapy, Dermal Fillers, and Muscle Relaxant treatments. If the demand for microdermabrasion treatment is high, you can purchase a second hand machine.

Clinics which use my consulting services have successfully managed to convert microdermabrasion requests to chemical peel treatments since the treatment results are superior and only nurses or physicians can administer higher concentrations of peels. In my opinion, microdermabrasion is a beauty salon treatment and is not a medical treatment. Employees of medical aesthetic practices should be trained to convert clients from less effective treatments such as microdermabrasion to medical grade chemical peel treatments with poise.

18 Years & Younger (American Society of Plastic Surgeons)

Cosmetic Procedures – Surgical	Patients-2006	% of total	% change
	18 and younger	18 and younger	2005 vs. 2006
Breast augmentation (Augmentation mammaplasty)	9,104	3%	12%
Breast implant removals (Augmentation patients only)	80	0%	0%
Breast lift (Mastopexy)	1,696	2%	-1%
Breast reduction in men (Gyneconmastia)	13,949	70%	21%
Chin augmentation (Mentoplasty)	1,357	9%	-15%
Dermabrasion	3,006	4%	-12%
Ear Surgery (Otoplasty)	9,930	33%	-8%
Eyelid Surgery (Blepharoplasty)	2,099	1%	-2%
Lip augmentation (other than injectable materials)	267	1%	-11%
Liposuction	4,721	2%	-4%
Nose reshaping (Rhinoplasty)	47,757	16%	-13%
TOTAL COSMETIC SURGICAL PROCEDURES	**93,966**	**5%**	**-6%**
Cosmetic Procedures - minimal-invasive			
Botox® injection	22,795	1%	3%
Chemical peel	4,119	0%	-9%
Laser hair removal	76,608	9%	11%
Laser skin resurfacing	11,519	4%	-17%
Laser treatment of leg veins	17,169	12%	-9%
Microdermabrasion	10,607	1%	15%
Sclerotherapy	3,317	1%	-11%
Soft tissue fillers			
Calcium hydroxylapatile (Radiance)	370	0%	0%
Collagen	1,223	0%	8%
Fat	446	1%	18%
Hyaluronic acid (Hylaform, Restylane)	1,233	0%	0%
Polylactic acid (Sculptra)	752	1%	0%
TOTAL COSMETIC MINIMAL-INVASIVE PROCEDURES	**150,158**	**2%**	**5%**
TOTAL COSMETIC PROCEDURES	**244,124**	**2%**	**1%**

This segment contributed 5% to the total surgical procedures for 2006. If you plan to include the 18 and under market in your promotional campaign, home in on chemical peels and cosmeceutical skin care since this target group's primary problem is acne. You may want to target the parents. For dentists and orthodontists whose database consists of young clients, this is a perfect opportunity to create an acne division with a comprehensive skin care division. TCA Peels and Glycolic Acid Peels are very effective in treating grade 1 to grade 3 acne. If the acne is severe, it is best to refer the client to a dermatologist. This is not a large market and a lot of resources should not be dedicated to attracting this target market into your practice if they are not already on the practice's database.

"Always think outside the box and embrace opportunities that appear, wherever they might be". Lakshmi Mittal

19-29 Years (American Society of Plastic Surgeons)

Cosmetic Procedures – Surgical	Patients- 2006	% of total	% change
	Ages 19-29	Ages 19-29	2005 vs. 2006
Breast augmentation (Augmentation mammaplasty)	95,474	29%	15%
Breast implant removals (Augmentation patients only)	2,761	10%	-4%
Breast lift (Mastopexy)	14,576	14%	11%
Breast reduction in men (Gyneconmastia)	2576	13%	37%
Buttock Lift	300	8%	-12%
Cheek implant (Malar augmentation)	782	9%	-4%
Chin augmentation (Mentoplasty)	1,929	13%	7%
Dermabrasion	3,471	5%	-18%
Ear Surgery (Otoplasty)	7,960	26%	20%
Eyelid Surgery (Blepharoplasty)	3,969	2%	-15%
Facelift (Rhytidectomy)	337	0%	0%
Forehead Lift	211	0%	9%
Hair transplantation	1,577	6%	-28%
Lip augmentation (other than injectable materials)	2,627	10%	-13%
Liposuction	38,028	13%	-10%
Lower body lift	772	7%	0%
Nose reshaping (Rhinoplasty)	87,459	28%	12%
Thigh lift	886	7%	
Tummy tuck (Abdominoplasty)	13,793	9%	24%
Upper arm lift	1,119	8%	17%
TOTAL COSMETIC SURGICAL PROCEDURES	**280,994**	**15%**	**8%**
Cosmetic Procedures - minimal-invasive			
Botox® injection	82,437	2%	11%
Cellulite treatment	7,059	21%	-22%
Chemical peel	11,820	1%	4%
Laser hair removal	249,984	28%	13%
Laser skin resurfacing	15,774	6%	-8%
Laser treatment of leg veins	20,994	15%	11%
Microdermabrasion	84,860	10%	2%
Sclerotherapy	28,402	5%	2%
Soft tissue fillers			
Calcium hydroxylapatile (Radiance)	1,960	2%	32%
Collagen	11,018	4%	23%
Fat	2,204	4%	-7%
Hyaluronic acid (Hylaform, Restylane)	13,420	2%	74%
Polylactic acid (Sculptura)	2,400	4%	28%
TOTAL COSMETIC MINIMAL-INVASIVE PROCEDURES	**532,334**	**6%**	**10%**
TOTAL COSMETIC PROCEDURES	**813,328**	**7%**	**9%**

37

2006 Cosmetic procedures- ages 19-29

2006 top five surgical procedures
Breast Augmentation
Nose reshaping
Liposuction
Breast lifts
Tummy tucks

2006 top five non-surgical procedures
Laser hair removal
Microdermabrasion
Botox® injection
Chemical peels

2006 surgical procedures with the highest growth
Breast Reduction in Men
Calf Augmentation
Ear Surgery
Upper Arm Lift
Thigh Lift

2006 non-surgical procedures with the highest growth
Hyaluronic Acid
Radiesse™
Sculptra®

This segment contributed 26% to the 2004 surgical procedure total and in 2006 its contribution has dropped to 15%. However, the top four procedures have risen from prior year which is important information for surgeons who target this market. Surgeons should home in on these procedures. While liposuction is a top procedure, its total has decreased from prior year. This target group is young and finance is a concern, so payment options such as interest free financing is important to attract this demographic. Transform Group, Harley Medical and most of the national groups attract this market segment by offering interest free financing and other cheesy promotions which appeal to this target market. It is very important that you understand your target market needs and not miss out on opportunities.

30-39 Years (American Society of Plastic Surgeons)

Cosmetic Procedures – Surgical	Patients-2006	% of total	% change
	Ages 30-39	Ages 30-39	2005 vs. 2006
Breast augmentation (Augmentation mammaplasty)	118,525	36%	9%
Breast implant removals (Augmentation patients only)	7,449	27%	4%
Breast lift (Mastopexy)	33,988	33%	11%
Breast reduction in men (Gyneconmastia)	1,615	8%	28
Buttock Lift	1,017	27%	-32%
Cheek implant (Malar augmentation)	1,565	18%	-4%
Chin augmentation (Mentoplasty)	1,965	13%	3%
Dermabrasion	7,045	11%	6%
Ear Surgery (Otoplasty)	5,523	18%	14%
Eyelid Surgery (Blepharoplasty)	13,155	6%	-15%
Facelift (Rhytidectomy)	1,897	2%	5%
Forehead Lift	2,318	4%	-24%
Hair transplantation	3,527	13%	-49%
Lip augmentation (other than injectable materials)	3,470	14%	5%
Liposuction	96,567	32%	-7%
Lower body lift	2,739	27%	11%
Nose reshaping (Rhinoplasty)	79,400	26%	10%
Thread lift	49,552	34%	12%
Tummy tuck (Abdominoplasty)	3,008	20%	44%
Upper arm lift	93	9%	31%
TOTAL COSMETIC SURGICAL PROCEDURES	**438,481**	**24%**	**4%**
Cosmetic Procedures - minimal-invasive			
Botox® injection	748,650	18%	9%
Cellulite treatment	18,488	55%	-22%
Chemical peel	119,177	11%	12%
Laser hair removal	246,758	28%	14%
Laser skin resurfacing	19,406	7%	0%
Laser treatment of leg veins	36,810	25%	-10%
Microdermabrasion	242,380	30%	-12%
Sclerotherapy	121,088	20%	-12%
Soft tissue fillers			
Calcium hydroxylapatile (Radiance)	8,096	10%	36%
Collagen	31,028	12%	14%
Fat	6,613	13%	15%
Hyaluronic acid (Hylaform, Restylane)	79,321	10%	52%
Polylactic acid (Sculptra)	5,754	10%	3%
TOTAL COSMETIC MINIMAL-INVASIVE PROCEDURES	**1,683,569**	**18%**	**5%**
TOTAL COSMETIC PROCEDURES	**2,122,050**	**19%**	**5%**

2006 Cosmetic procedures- ages 30-39

2006 top five surgical procedures
Breast augmentation
Liposuction
Nose reshaping
Tummy Tuck
Eyelid Surgery

2006 top five non-surgical procedures
Botox® injection
Laser hair removal
Microdermabrasion
Sclerotherapy
Chemical peels
Dermal fillers

2006 surgical procedures with the highest growth
Breast reduction in men
Vaginal rejuvenation
Upper arm lift
Thigh lift

2006 non-surgical procedure with the highest growth
Chemical peels
Laser hair removal
Radiesse™
Hyaluronic Acid

This market segment contribution to 2004 surgical total was 38% and a 46% contribution to the 2004 procedure total. The statistics has now shifted downward to 24% contribution to surgical procedures and 19% contribution to procedure total. This is a dramatic downward shift from the 2004 figures. The non-surgical figures have remained flat from previous year. The results indicate that this market's contribution to surgical treatments is still powerful but the trend shows clients prefer non-surgical/holistic treatments to surgical treatments. In my opinion, a surgeon should use non-surgical treatments such as Chemical Peels, Mesotherapy and Botox to pull this market into their practices. Once there is face to face contact, the practice has a better opportunity to educate the client on the benefits of surgical procedures and other higher priced procedures.

40-54 Years (American Society of Plastic Surgeons)

Cosmetic Procedures – Surgical	Patients-2006	% of total	% change
	ages 40-54	ages 40-54	2005 vs. 2006
Breast augmentation (Augmentation mammaplasty)	90,563	27%	17%
Breast implant removals (Augmentation patients only)	12,008	44%	16%
Breast lift (Mastopexy	40,285	39%	11%
Breast reduction in men (Gyneconmastia)	1,258	6%	13%
Buttock Lift	1,815	49%	-26%
Cheek implant (Malar augmentation)	3,746	43%	-16%
Chin augmentation (Mentoplasty)	3,392	23%	0%
Dermabrasion	22,331	32%	7%
Ear Surgery (Otoplasty)	3,860	13%	20%
Eyelid Surgery (Blepharoplasty)	99,047	42%	0%
Facelift (Rhytidectomy)	33,936	33%	-10%
Forehead Lift	22,251	42%	-9%
Hair transplantation	8,151	29%	-47%
Lip augmentation (other than injectable materials)	9,076	35%	-11%
Liposuction	126,350	42%	-4%
Lower body lift	5,162	50%	-3%
Nose reshaping (Rhinoplasty)	65,403	21%	-3%
Thigh lift	6,628	54%	27%
Thread lift	2,322	44%	22%
Tummy tuck (Abdominoplasty)	62,363	43%	7%
Upper arm lift	6,099	41%	23%
TOTAL COSMETIC SURGICAL PROCEDURES	**627,027**	**34%**	**1%**
Cosmetic Procedures - minimal-invasive			
Botox® injection	2,245,286	55%	8%
Cellulite treatment	7,731	23%	-22%
Chemical peel	455,720	43%	0%
Laser hair removal	260,467	29%	13%
Laser skin resurfacing	116,564	44%	-2%
Laser treatment of leg veins	45,487	31%	-6%
Microdermabrasion	328,831	40%	-1%
Sclerotherapy	310,623	51%	7%
Soft tissue fillers			
Calcium hydroxylapatile (Radiance)	31,095	39%	23%
Collagen	106,044	40%	28%
Fat	19,684	37%	12%
Hyaluronic acid (Hylaform, Restylane)	372,023	48%	59%
Polylactic acid (Sculptra)	32,752	60%	25%
TOTAL COSMETIC MINIMAL-INVASIVE PROCEDURES	**4,332,307**	**47%**	**10%**
TOTAL COSMETIC PROCEDURES	**4,959,334**	**45%**	**9%**

41

2006 Cosmetic procedures- ages 40 and 54

2006 top five surgical procedures
Liposuction
Breast Augmentation
Eyelid surgery
Nose reshaping
Tummy tucks

2006 top five non-surgical procedures
Botox® injections
Chemical peels
Hyaluronic acid (Restylane)
Microdermabrasion
Sclerotherapy

2006 surgical procedure with the highest growth
Calf Augmentation
Vaginal rejuvenation
Pectoral implants
Thread lift
Thigh lift
Upper arm lift

2006 non- surgical procedures with the highest growth
Hyaluronic Acid
Collagen
Sculptra®

This target market is now the largest contributor to surgical and non-surgical procedures with significant increase in all top procedures including Muscle Relaxant treatments. As is indicated above, the top surgical and non-surgical procedures are similar within all target groups. Some surgical and non-surgical procedures are more popular among the different markets.

Age distribution – 55+ years (American Society of Plastic Surgeons)

Cosmetic Procedures – Surgical	Patients-2006	% of total	% change
	Ages 55+	Ages 55+	2005 vs 2006
Breast augmentation (Augmentation mammaplasty)	15,730	5%	13%
Breast implant removals (Augmentation patients only)	5,153	19%	22%
Breast lift (Mastoopexy)	13,315	13%	21%
Breast reduction in men (Gyneconmastia)	482	2%	5%
Buttock Lift	578	16%	-36%
Cheek implant (Malar augmentation)	2,709	31%	13%
Chin augmentation (Mentoplasty)	6,006	41%	-7%
Dermabrasion	33,087	48%	-3%
Ear Surgery (Otoplasty)	2,864	10%	14%
Eyelid Surgery (Blepharoplasty)	115,203	49%	5%
Facelift (Rhytidectomy)	67,895	65%	-1%
Forehead Lift	27,745	53%	0%
Hair transplantation	14,610	52%	-37%
Lip augmentation (other than injectable materials)	10,186	40%	13%
Liposuction	37,122	12%	-8%
Lower body lift	1,650	16%	28%
Nose reshaping (Rhinooplasty)	27,239	9%	5%
Thigh lift	1,819	15%	48%
Thread lift	2,453	47%	29%
Tummy tuck (Abdominoplasty)	20,532	14%	21%
Upper arm lift			
TOTAL COSMETIC SURGICAL PROCEDURES	**411,541**	**22%**	**1%**
Cosmetic Procedures – minimal-invasive			
Botox® injection	991,348	24%	1%
Cellulite treatment	336	1%	-22%
Chemical peel	472,588	44%	4%
Laser hair removal	53,222	6%	16%
Laser skin resurfacing	99,661	38%	-2%
Laser treatment of leg veins	24,167	17%	-14%
Microdermabrasion	150,095	18%	9%
Sclerotherapy	143,636	24%	10%
Soft tissue fillers			
Calcium hydroxylapatile (Radiance)	37,327	47%	13%
Collagen	118,026	44%	18%
Fat	23,957	45%	5%
Hyaluronic acid (Hylaform, Restylane)	312,288	40%	62%
Sculptra	13,254	24%	18%
TOTAL COSMETIC MINIMAL-INVASIVE PROCEDURES			
TOTAL COSMETIC PROCEDURES	**2,851,446**	**26%**	**8%**

43

2006 Cosmetic procedures- ages 55+

2006 top surgical procedure
Eyelid surgery
Facelifts
Dermabrasion
Liposuction
Forehead lift

2006 top non-surgical procedures
Botox® injections
Chemical peels
Hyaluronic Acid
Microdermabrasion
Sclerotherapy

2006 surgical procedure with the highest growth
Breast augmentation
Breast lift
Breast implant removal
Calf Augmentation
Lower Body Lift
Thigh lift
Thread lift
Upper arm lift
Vaginal rejuvenation

2006 non surgical procedures with the highest growth
Hyaluronic Acid
Radiesse™
Sculptra®
Sclerotherapy

This market segment contributed only 7% to 2004 non-surgical totals procedures. Now its contribution has increased to 27% indicating that this market is continually shifting towards non-surgical procedures for their enhancement needs. Had surgeons expanded their practices to include non-surgical treatments earlier, they could have slowed down the clear division that exists between surgical practices and non-surgical practices in the United Kingdom.

2006 Statistical Data Summary
Procedure demand by age group

2006 Top Procedures	Ages 20-29	Ages 30-39	Ages 40-54	Ages 55+
Breast augmentation	95,474	118,525	90,653	15,730
Breast lift	14,503	33,988	40,285	13,315
Ear Surgery (Otoplasty)	7,960	5,523	3,860	2,864
Eyelid Surgery (Blepharoplasty)	3,696	13,155	99,047	115,203
Facelift (Rhytidectomy)	337	1,897	33,926	67,895
Forehead lift	211	2,318	22,251	27,745
Hair transplantation	1,577	3,527	8,151	14,610
Lip augmentation (surgical)	2,627	3,470	9,076	10,186
Liposuction	38,028	96,567	126,350	37,122
Nose reshaping (Rhinoplasty)	87,459	79,400	65,403	27,239
Tummy tuck	13,793	49,552	62,363	20,532
Botox® injection	82,437	748,650	2,245,286	991,348
Chemical peel	11,820	119,117	455,720	472,588
Laser hair removal	294,984	246,748	260,467	53,222
Laser treatment of leg veins	20,994	36,810	45,487	24,167
Laser skin resurfacing	15,776	19,406	116,564	99,661
Microdermabrasion	84,860	242,380	328,831	150,095
Sclerotherapy	28,402	121,008	310,623	143,636
Collagen	11,018	31,028	106,044	118,226
Hyaluronic acid (Hylaform, Restylane)	13,420	79,321	372,023	312,288
Radiesse	1,960	8,096	31,095	37,397
Sculptra	2,400	5,754	32,752	13,254

"When people talk about successful businesses and those that are not so successful, the customer determines at the end of the day who is successful and for what reason". Gerry Harvey

2006 Market Segment Summary

Segments	Surgical % change 2005 vs. 2006	Surgical % of total	Non Surgical % change 2005 vs. 2006	Non Surgical % of total
Male Market	-10	14	-7	10
Female Market	4	86	9	90
18 and under	-6	5	1	2
19-29 age group	8	15	9	6
30-39 age group	4	24	5	18
40-55 age group	1	34	10	47
55+ age group	1	22	9	27

Chart 1 gives you a visual overview of the popular procedures among the different market segments, and chart 2 shows at a glance the market segments with the highest contribution to the 2006 total procedures. At this point, I strongly recommend that you look at your market and segment your entire base into smaller segments as is indicated in the charts. Identify the top five procedures in each segment. You will need to gather local demographic information by typing into Google (demographics and your place of residence). Procedure choices (provided in the book) and local area demographics statistics will give you a great head start in identifying your core markets and their aesthetic needs.

Now work with your PR department to create a more focused promotional message for each segment. Focused means create individual advertisement for each procedure. For instance, if a surgeon wants to increase the volume of facelift procedures, create an enticing facelift advertisement stating the benefits of the procedure to the target audience. Make powerful statements regarding down time since this is a concern to everyone. The surgeon's promotion department may want to clearly indicate the cost effectiveness of choosing a face lift over non-surgical treatments to treat sagging skin which may require surgery. The PR agent may want to assess the cost of combination treatments of Botox, Fillers, Sculptra, Thermage and IPL to improve one's appearance instead of choosing a facelift option.

Place the advertisement in the appropriate promotional medium which targets the 50+ age group. This type of targeted message on the benefits of just one procedure which is of interest to the appropriate target market will generate a greater response than placing an advertisement listing the surgeon's entire range of services. Equally, the PR consultant can use the information provided to create a range of focused advertisements for a number of key procedures. When this activity is completed, test the ads to evaluate their effectiveness. Test means find cheap and easy ways to see whether the promotional message works. For example, to test a mailer, create a targeted message and mail to a small list of existing clients. If the response rate is poor, redesign the advertisement. If the response rate is higher than average, create a larger scale mailing list.

A primary objective of this section of the book is to supply the reader with all the information needed for a creative PR agency to design awe-inspiring targeted messages to the specific market segment. Select experience PR consultants who know what they are doing. They should be skilled in target marketing. If this section of the book is utilized effectively, the clinic's promotional message to the local market will be more targeted, outperforming its competitors and ultimately attracting more potential clients into the practice.

National Plastic Surgery Statistics	National 2004 Surgeon Fee	National 2006 Surgeon Fee	2006 Total Expenditure
Breast augmentation (Augmentation mammaplasty)	$3373	$3600	$1,185,920,285
Breast implant removals (Augmentation patients only)	$2211	$2319	$63,669,776
Breast lift (Mastopexy)	$3718	$4220	$437,952,317
Breast reduction in men (Gyneconmastia)	$2812	$3124	$62,108,293
Buttock Lift	$3630	$4527	$16,796,076
Cheek implant (Malar augmentation)	$1854	$2,279	$20,060,863
Chin augmentation (Mentoplasty)	$1512	$1910	$27,983,274
Dermabrasion	$866	$951	$65,899,805
Ear Surgery (Otoplasty)	$2339	$2388	$71,967,156
Eyelid Surgery (Bblepharoplasty)	$2523	$2,877	$670,978,018
Facelift (Rhytidectomy)	$4822	$4856	$505,305,441
Forehead Lift	$2400	$2846	$149,483,588
Lip Augmentation (other than injectables)	$1199	$1603	$41,074,423
Liposuction	$2223	$2750	$832,747,086
Lower body lift	$6425	$7578	$78,229,506
Nose reshaping (Rhinoplasty)	$3332	$3841	$1180,064,233
Thigh lift	$3857	$4376	$53,806,950
Tummy tuck (Abdominoplasty)	$4505	$5,063	$740,343,243
Upper arm lift	$3106	$3513	$52,293,458
TOTAL COSMETIC SURGICAL PROCEDURES			
Cosmetic Procedures - minimal-invasive			
Botox® injection	$376	$492	$2,011,283,275
Cellulite treatment	$127	$192	$6,453,888
Chemical peel	$607	$686	$729,527,236
Laser hair removal	$428	$466	$412,970,414
Laser skin resurfacing	$2117	$2160	$567,947,705
Laser treatment of leg veins	$346	$400	$57,876,537
Microdermabrasion	$173	$264	$215,959,054
Sclerotherapy	$322	$332	$201,446,347
Soft tissue fillers			
Calcium hydroxylapatile (Radiance)	$901	$810	$63,899,055
Collagen	$368	$390	$104,359,120
Fat	$1226	$1380	$72,982,096
Hyaluronic acid (Hylaform, Restylane)	$539	$585	$455,217,308
Polylactic acid (Sculptra)		$1042	$57,240,587
TOTAL COSMETIC MINIMAL-INVASIVE PROCEDURES			
2006 Total Cosmetic Procedures			**$11,355,870,657**
2004 Total Cosmetic Procedures			**$8,403,557,322**

Marketing involves the skill of knowing your customers and customizing products and services to meet your customers' needs. The information provided in section 1.2 gives you extensive knowledge of the different segments and their procedure preference. It is apparent the different segments prefer similar procedures, however, their preference for certain procedures increase or decrease as these individuals age. The desire for more surgical and non-surgical treatments increases as one age. For example, the 30-39 age group procedure preference is similar to the 19-29 age group. The trend shows that the average female is postponing childbirth into their thirties. Therefore, the desire for breast lift and tummy tuck is higher for the 30-39 age group. Similarly, Botox, Fillers, Sclerotheapy, and Chemical Peels have increased in popularity for the 30-39 age group.

If your local demographics study indicates that the 30-39 average household income is below the country's national average, there is a chance that this segment might be price sensitive. Therefore, you may want to state that your clinic provides interest free credit in your advertisement. You may want to contact finance agencies such as Medenta Finance (www.medenta.com) to become a lending broker for the company. The company will take on the lending risk for a fee, and you can transfer this cost into the price of the procedure. It is essential to offer credit options in this business since most market segments rely on credit to finance most of their discretionary purchases.

You will stand out if your communication message to these segments is precise-you must communicate to the different groups as if you know them intimately.

Market segmentation will benefit the practice as follows:

- Better matching of clients' needs

- Enhanced profit

- Better opportunity for growth

- Retain more clients

Knowing your market segments and improving your communication message is vital in attracting new clients into the practice. However this skill is not enough to keep customers returning to the practice. Section 1.3 discusses the key elements of technical training. Providing popular treatment is not enough to achieve long term success. You must become an expert in the treatments that you provide and effective training and development are essential.

1.3 Training and Development

Before I begin to discuss the different types of training organizations which exist in the United Kingdom, Europe, and United States I want to share with you my interpretation of the skill sets required to become an enhancement consultant to the medical aesthetic and anti-ageing market.

How do we define outer beauty?

To most individuals, a face is considered beautiful if there is:

- Youthfulness
- Fresh complexion
- Beautiful smile with healthy teeth and gums
- Facial symmetry
- Large ascending eyes
- Beautiful lips
- High cheekbones

Special contribution from Professor Syed Haq

Specialists such as Plastic Surgeons and Cosmetic Dentists may use measurements such as Phi (1.618) to determine facial imperfections including the teeth. The golden ratio, also known as the divine proportion or Phi (phi – Φ) is a mathematical constant equal to 1.6180339887 and has been described in mathematics and the arts for many centuries as being typically defined by the division of a line, for example, such that the ratio of the longer to the shorter segment is

1.618:1. This ratio has been identified as an aesthetic ideal and is still observed today as a guiding principle.

The golden ratio has many applications and for that matter, has continued to intrigue intellectuals for millennia. It has strongly been believed by the ancient Greeks, historians, artists, scientists and architects that Π has a role in every element that surrounds us, from music, art, wildlife, natural and man-made structures to aesthetics. The use of the golden ratio as a tool in aesthetics probably dates back to 300 B.C. by Euclid of Alexandria and then later in 1509 where Luca Paciola published his findings entitled "De Divina Proportione", in which the mathematics of the golden ratio or divine proportion was first truly explored and defined.

A longstanding question in aesthetics is "What is beauty?" Is beauty only in the eye of the beholder, or are there some absolute values? "I know not what beauty is, but I know that it touches many things", Dürer. Understanding the golden ratio can at least in part help the aesthetic specialist in improving their ability to achieve improved facial aesthetic outcomes when treating their patients. Phi can allow the specialist to focus their attention on relative proportionality.

Developed by Dr. Craig Shrosbree (Rejuvadent-Grimbsy) with written contribution from Professor Syed Haq.

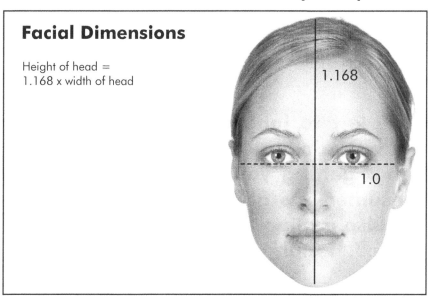

Facial Dimensions

Height of head =
1.168 x width of head

1.168

1.0

Facial Dimensions. The Phi constant A. The picture demonstrates a "perfect" face and how the proportions of the head (height and width) conform to certain mathematical measurements that relate to the golden ratio (∏).

Professional make-up artists and other enhancement specialists with an understanding of proportionality and balance will apply their technical skills to improve facial imperfections. Therefore, if the width of a person's face is not in proportion to the length of the head, a skilled make-up artist will know how to use colour and sculpting techniques to achieve balance to the face resulting in a more attractive and symmetrical face. In addition, talented hairdressers can achieve similar results by using an alternative approach which can bring greater balance and proportionality to the face. Unfortunately, very few medical aesthetic training companies understand and are aware of proportionality and facial balance.

Non-surgical medicine is a very new and developing arm of the enhancement industry. The majority of non-surgical specialists presently in the industry, except for plastic surgeons and dentists, do not understand proportionality/balance, and have in the main been successful despite providing a somewhat inferior service to the public. As this industry becomes more competitive, there is and will continue to be greater pressures placed on the need to attract new, and maintain, existing business. It will therefore, be an absolute pre-requisite for aesthetic practitioners to have the highest standards of training to deliver a higher level of expertise in facial assessment. Clients will demand much more of their enhancement specialists.

"The key to longevity is to keep doing what you do better than anyone else. It's about getting your message out to the consumer. It's about getting their trust, but also getting them excited, again and again". Ralph Lauren

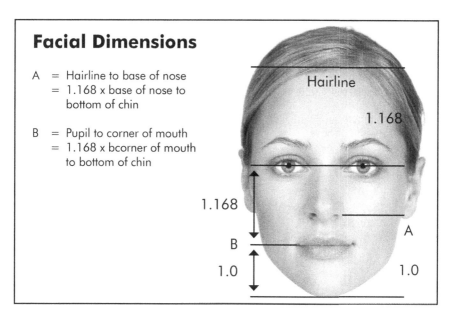

Facial Dimensions

A = Hairline to base of nose
   = 1.168 x base of nose to bottom of chin

B = Pupil to corner of mouth
   = 1.168 x bcorner of mouth to bottom of chin

Hairline

1.168

1.168

B

1.0

A

1.0

Facial Dimensions. B. External Dimensions. The picture demonstrates a "perfect" face and how various proportions taken from differing points of the head (level of the hairline), eye (lateral canthus), base of the nose, mid lip line and base of the chin can give rise to the concept of Phi.

Facial Dimensions

Width at temple =
1.168 x outer width of eyes

Width of mouth =
1.168 x width of nose

Facial Dimensions. C. Internal Dimensions. The picture demonstrates a "perfect" face and how internal proportions taken from differing points of the head (level of the temple – supra-orbital), eye (lateral canthus), and widest part of the nose (base), upper lip line (level of the philtrum) further validate the concept of Phi

Facial Dimensions

Face is devided equally into thirds

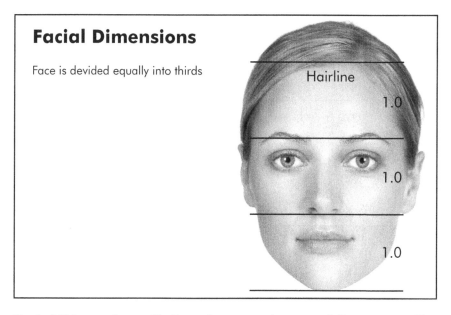

Hairline

1.0

1.0

1.0

Facial Dimensions. D. Equal proportions and Symmetry. The picture demonstrates a "perfect" face and how face can be divided equally in to thirds from the hairline, temple, base of the nose and chin can further validate the concept of Phi.

Understanding facial dimensions and how changing one or more areas of a face can affect the overall relative facial proportions and therefore, Phi will be an important lesson for all aesthetic specialists to be fully in tune with so as to later, refine and bring balance to a client's face.

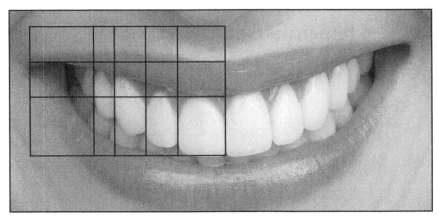

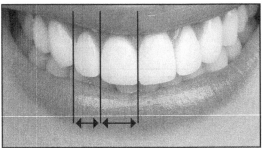
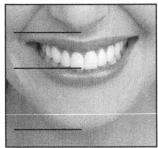

Dental Dimensions. Upper Panel. The PhiDental Grid developed by PhiMatrix (devised by Dr Eddy Levin) allows the cosmetic dentist and orthodontist to apply the principles of golden proportions in determining a standardised treatment program for their patients.

Lower Left Panel- In this panel we see that the central incisor width to the adjacent lateral incisor width is in a golden ratio. This relationship also extends to the canine and premolar teeth.

Lower Right Panel - In a relaxed face the bottom of the nose to the bottom of the chin may be divided into two portions by the "lip line", where the distance between the lip line and lower chin is in a golden proportion with the distance between the lip line and base of the nose (exemplified by the Golden Mean Gauge).

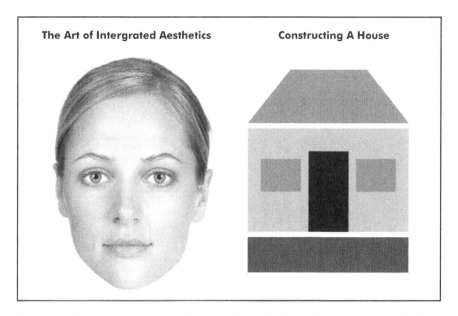

The Art of Intergrated Aesthetics   **Constructing A House**

The art of integrated aesthetics uses the principle that when considering any aesthetic issue the specialist must not only acknowledge proportions but at all times consider the face in its entirety. This should therefore, include the layers that make up the structure of the face, much like when constructing a house from its very foundations.

Analogy is highlighted:

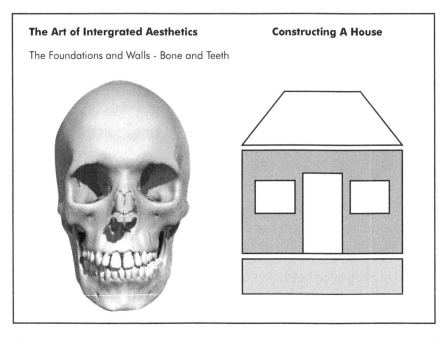

The Art of Intergrated Aesthetics   **Constructing A House**

The Foundations and Walls - Bone and Teeth

The bones of the skull and teeth which provide the first layer of structural integrity of any face are comparable to the foundations and walls of a house under construction.

The Art of Intergrated Aesthetics

The Foundations and Walls - Bone and Teeth

Constructing A House

The Plaster - Muscle and soft tissue

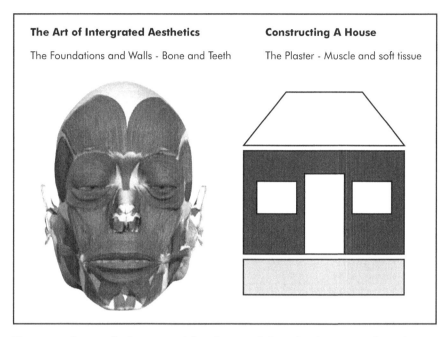

The muscles, soft tissue and fascia overlying the bone and teeth are in effect, like the plaster found on the walls of a house.

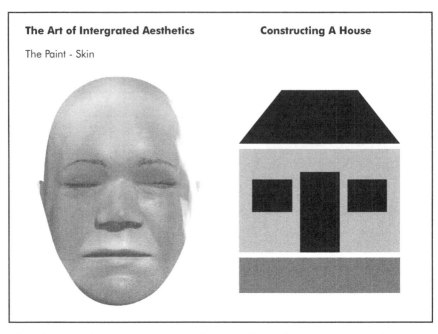

The Art of Intergrated Aesthetics   **Constructing A House**

The Paint - Skin

The skin overlying the various layers of the face is akin to the paint found on the walls of a house.

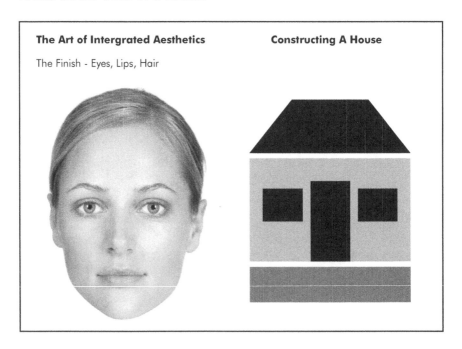

The Art of Intergrated Aesthetics   **Constructing A House**

The Finish - Eyes, Lips, Hair

Finally, the eyes, lips and hair are the final finishing touches required much like the finish to a house. The building of layer upon layer in an integrated way of a person's face should always be at the forefront of any aesthetic specialist when deciding on a treatment plan for their patient. The analytical processing should be an integrated part of the specialists' repertoire.

It should be noted that there are no absolutes in life. "Symmetry is a principal determinant of aesthetic preference. Perceptual organisational processes may also be more important in guiding aesthetic choice even more so than a unique mathematical proportion" (Davis and Jahnke, 1991).

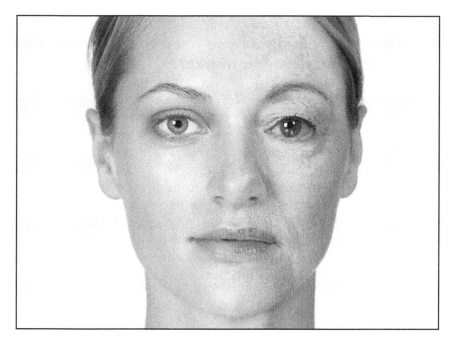

Regardless of how beautiful and well proportioned a face may appear, ageing will compromise facial dimensions and underlying facial structures creating a less attractive external appearance. A skilled clinician needs to be familiar with the effects of internal and external ageing and its impact on the underlying facial structure to set realistic expectations for the client. At present, ninety percent of non-surgical specialists are unfamiliar with facial proportionality and facial anatomy and continue to rely on patients instructions of what needs to be done.

My 14 years of experience working with cosmetic clients has led me to the following conclusions: 1) cosmetic clients do not desire a particular treatment such as Botox®. The client's request is based on his/her belief that the benefits associated with the treatment will make him/her look better. 2) the demand for cosmetic treatments is perpetuated by the desire to enhance one's appearance. Cosmetic clients expect the clinician to be skilled in aesthetic medicine. 3) In most cases, the solution will involve multiple procedures.

New clinicians entering this market should not focus on just Botox and Dermal Fillers as their treatment offering. The use of these two procedures in most cases cannot improve one's overall appearance even for the very young.

What level of training do you need to compete in the present medical aesthetic market?

If your practice was established a decade ago, providing just Botulinum Toxin treatments could have earned you a healthy living. Earning a healthy living does not mean that you are skilled. It could mean that you are lucky to be in a business at a time when there are few competitors. Today there are more suppliers of Botulinum Toxin treatments than there are clients to go around. Therefore, it is almost impossible for one to earn a mediocre income by providing Botulinum Toxin treatment alone. At the beginning of the book, I stated that as the industry becomes more competitive, which it is, clinicians' technical skills will have to improve exponentially to motivate existing clients to remain loyal to their practices.

The market has evolved and cosmetic clients no longer want non-surgical clinicians who will react to their request. Cosmetic clients prefer to deal with non-surgical experts who can communicate effectively, who can assess their needs, who are artistic, and who can provide top notch treatment results. New clinicians wanting to take market share from existing competitors need to be well trained, and it is for this reason that we developed K-T Training in 2005.

I might be biased, but I do believe that K-T Training is the only company that teaches the integrated approach of non-surgical medicine. The company has hired specialists including dentists, dermatologists, and surgeons to develop and refine its integrated approach in non-surgical medicine. Also, the company's owners are specialists in IT, Web Marketing and Global Marketing. The owners of the company are accomplished business consultants who have created successful clinics in the United Kingdom and throughout North America. We generously provide business guidance to candidates at no cost. Since the company has a strong business management division, we feel that whenever past trainees excel in the market, K-T Training also excels because it is K-T Training business expertise and the trainee's motivation which work hand in hand to make the new project a success.

Independent Training Companies

Regardless of which training company you choose, you should not make your decision on price alone. This is your future career so do not compromise on your development. Choose a company with the following credentials:

- The training company is not associated with the manufacturer.
- The company has expert trainers for each procedure. Very rarely does one clinician have the expertise to teach every procedure.
- Be very careful of training companies that provide training as a part time business to supplement their income. There are many clinicians providing training to supplement their income and you need to ask why they need to supplement their income if they are true experts. Be aware of distributor/training companies who will most probably train you on the product they distribute which may not be the best product in its category.

- Evaluate if the chosen company is successful in medical aesthetics and evaluate their contribution in the industry. As mentioned earlier, 90% of clinicians are not properly trained in medical aesthetics. It is not uncommon that one of these clinicians might be your trainer.

- If the company promises marketing resources, find out what they provide. In most cases, you will need help with your strategy, brochure scripts, web script, how to negotiate with salons, etc....................

63

■   List all your marketing questions and find out if they provide solutions to these challenges. By questioning the person on the phone, you will be able to identify if you are dealing with people who know the business.

Manufacture's Training

Most manufacturer training will be biased since the manufacturer's objective is to persuade you to use only their range of products as a complete solution. In the majority of manufacturer's led training courses, the training does not teach you the skill of assessing the client's face holistically and providing multiple treatment options to reach the desired results. Most of the training courses that I have evaluated, and I have evaluated many, are not detailed enough to prepare you for everyday scenarios that you will encounter.

For example, if I were coordinating a technique session for clinicians, I would select clients that are healthy, with great skin tone and elasticity, and younger clients who only need my product to enhance their appearance. However, in real life, most clients need multiple solutions and in most cases the results they are hoping to achieve are unrealistic with the use of just a single product or procedure.

For example, if a client requested dermal fillers for her nasolabial folds but her skin is dehydrated, hyper pigmented, and lacks tone and elasticity, the outcome from treating the nasolabial(s) will most probably not meet the client's expectations. Remember, most clients are seeking treatments to enhance their overall appearance and in most cases the client believes that the removal of lines on their lower or upper face will achieve this outcome. However, in most cases the client will not look better if the client has other imperfections such as poor quality skin.

In the nasolabial scenario, you need the proper training to identify if the requested treatment will achieve the results the client is expecting. Therefore, I recommend that you do not reactively provide a treatment without identifying the client's objective. If the client's treatment request cannot achieve his/her objective, discuss the combination of treatments that will provide the results the client wants.

In the nasolabial scenario, the best approach of treatment might be a series of chemical peels before the dermal filler treatment. It is best that you discuss your recommendations and provide the client with all the options. If the client chooses to go with a dermal filler alternative and the result is not as expected, she will not be disappointed with your service but with her decision not to accept your recommendation.

Clinicians who passively react to clients' demands without making an attempt to discuss the complete solutions with their clients are providing a disservice to their clients. Clinicians trained by companies with a one-dimensional approach to aesthetic medicine will react to clients' requests. This response by clinicians is common and makes practices vulnerable to losing clients to the hundreds of other practices in the area.

Potential clients do not understand that the results they read about are not necessarily the results they will achieve, because their face is different from the models or the writer of the article. You will need to improve your communication skills quickly since the larger manufacturers are now using mass media to promote their products, therefore, a lot of new clients will request a particular product or procedure and if the request is not appropriate for the client, you need to be prepared on how to deal with this situation.

For example, Allergan and Q-Med are now engaging in mass media advertising to increase awareness on the benefits of their dermal filler products. The model in these advertisements are young and the benefits promised by the advertisement is vague. Therefore it is the clinician's responsibility to identify if Juvederm or Restylane alone will achieve the results the client is looking for.

"It is fundamental that you o help your clients to understand their individual needs".

Congresses

Congresses are a great way to find out what is new in the industry and to get together with other clinicians. In most cases, congresses are held in great locations and therefore the trip can be combined with a holiday. However, if funds are limited, you are better off using the funds to develop yourself. The best approach is to work with a company such as K-T Training to identify your goals and aspiration, and to develop a plan consisting of technical development and business development to improve your immediate and long term success. The congress fee can be put to better use toward your development and ultimate long term success. Remember to look at statistics before you make any buying decision.

 The best approach in developing your technical skills is to find a mentor. Someone who is established and has superior technical skills in the procedure you are interested in. Organize to have him/her come to your practice for a day, evening or weekend, to help you advance your technique skills. You should also spend some time in your mentor's practice to evaluate his/her entire business operation. Observe best practices in all areas of the practice and not just his/her technical skills.

K-T Training does provide a mentorship program (there is a fee for this service) for its candidates and other who may need further development. Information can be found on our site at www.kttraining.co.uk or e-mail us at info@kttraining.co.uk.

Communication Skills

Understanding Your Communication Style

Good communication skills require a high level of self-awareness. Understanding your personal style of communicating will go a long way towards helping you to create good and lasting impressions on others. By becoming more aware of how others perceive you, you can adapt more readily to their styles of communicating. This does not mean you have to be a chameleon, changing with every personality you meet. Instead, you can make another person more comfortable with you by selecting and emphasizing certain behaviour that fit within your personality and resonates with others.

There are three basic communication styles:
- Aggressive
- Passive
- Assertive

Discovering which style best fits you can be done in a number of ways including personality tests such as the Myers-Briggs Type Indicator (MBTI), psychological assessments, and self-assessments. Remaining aware of your own communication style and understanding your cosmetic client's communication style will help you to make your clients more comfortable with you-thus improving the communication between you and the client. Most cosmetic clients are sensitive about their appearance which is why they are coming to see you. The more diplomatic you are in discussing the client's needs without offending the individual, the better you will become at discussing and selling treatment programs. Fine-tuning this skill as time goes by gives you the best chance of success in growing your practice to million-dollar status.

In the previous section, I stated that the most common mistake made by cosmetic clinician is setting unrealistic expectation for the client for the following reasons; 1) the clinician reacted to the client's request without identifying what the client wanted to achieve and 2) the clinician does not have the ability to communicate or assess the client's needs.

Communication skill is essential if you plan to run a successful practice and sell multiple procedures in one consultation. In today's competitive market where most clinicians have to provide free consultations, it is essential that clinicians are effective in bonding with clients in the first meeting. In most cases, medical professionals are not effective in this area so training is required.

Case Study 1

Clinic One:

Place Advertisement in Local Newspaper for Muscle Relaxant and Dermal Fillers

Advertisement Cost: £700
Response: 10 consultations booked for Muscle Relaxant

Consultation Result: 3 booked for Muscle Relaxant treatment

Consultation cost is £233.33/patient

Average Gross Margin per procedure is £200/treatment

Results		Total
	3 patients treated resulting in a Gross margin of £600 The advertisement cost £700.00 The result is a loss of £100	£600
Cost of AD		£700
Net Results		£ (100)

Clinic Two

Place Advertisement in Local Newspaper for Muscle Relaxant and Dermal Fillers

Advertisement Cost: £700
Response: 10 consultations booked for Muscle Relaxant

Consultation Result: 5 Booked for multiple procedures

Consultation cost is £140/patient
Average Gross margin from procedure is £200/treatment

Results	Profit from Treatment	Total
	£400 gross margin- Muscle Relaxant and Fillers/ x5	£2000
Cost of AD	£140x5	£700
Net Results		£1,300

Consultation Booked:

If your consultation closing ratio is low, get business advice on ways to improve your communication skills immediately since this is the most common area for business failure.

Leadership Skills

In general medical professionals, predominantly physicians, dentists, and surgeons do not take a leadership position in their everyday business operation. They leave this to the Practice Manager who in most cases is not trained to run a sophisticated relationship marketing business like the structure I am proposing. I understand that the clinician is also the prime money earner, but it goes without saying that in private medicine, the business owner must understand every aspect of the business's daily operation, and must take on the additional responsibilities of making sure that the business is being managed for long term growth and profit.

The skills required by the business owner have to be superior to that of an NHS run operation where patients are handed to you and must use your services, regardless of service and patient satisfaction. Do not delegate this role to an office manager or another employee. If you are stressed or lack business skills, hire someone from the outside to assist you in mapping out your business strategy. Within the organization, the physician must be seen as the individual that assumes the role of commander and chief.

Our one day business management course provides the practice owner, and his/her management team, with fundamental business leadership training. Dr. Ilori and I (lecturers and course developer) have developed modules which can be integrated into your practice immediately and which will move the practice to a more customer centric model. Leadership and management training will give you the skill sets to rally your team together to accomplish the practice's long-term goals. Do not leave this responsibility to someone else.

For more information on leadership and business training for you and your management team, contact:

K-T Training at info@kttraining.co.uk or visit our website at www.k-tsloutions.com for business training information.

Useful Reading

The following books are written by experts in the industry of aesthetic medicine and I urge you to read these books as part of your self-development.

Manual of Chemical Peels: Superficial and Medium Depth

By Mark G Rubin

University of California, San Diego

Synopsis

This is a concise, highly practical manual on the chemical treatment of photo-aged skin covering superficial and medium peels. Authoritatively written, this practical guide provides an introduction to how peels work and discuss various peeling agents and treatment plans. It also provides detailed instruction on performing peels and covers post-peel care and maintenance. The Manual of Chemical Peels contains over 100 images — 60 in full colour — that clearly depict how a patient's skin improves. Includes sample consent and patient information forms.

Cosmetic Dermatology: Principles and Practice

By Leslie S. Baumann Editorial Reviews

University of Miami, Florida

Synopsis

This book begins with the anatomy and physiology of skin and proceeds to the science of basic skin conditions such as aging, dry skin and sensitive skin, as well as skin diseases such as acne. The next section covers cosmetic agents used in anti ageing, exfoliating, moisturizing, for sun and antioxidants. Cosmetic procedures follow. The book ends with information on selected non-invasive procedures that can be performed in an office setting, as well as a chapter on the psychosocial aspects of cosmetic dermatology. All of the very latest drugs and topical agents will be discussed including retinoid, moisturizing agents, antioxidants and depigmenting agents. Cosmetic procedures covered include soft tissue augmentation, chemical peel and hair removal methods and there is a chapter comparing cosmetic agents with drugs. Wherever possible, information is based on hard science.

The text aims to create a link, featuring a better flow of information, between the fields of dermatology and cosmetic science. Designed to help cosmetic dermatologists understand the information on various cosmetic products and procedures. Colour illustrations are included.

Age-less: The Definitive Guide to Botox, Collagen, Lasers, Peels, and Other Solutions for Flawless Skin

By Dr. Fred Brandt

Review from Publishers Weekly

Brandt, a New York and Miami dermatologist, and Reynoso, senior beauty editor at W magazine, offer a guidebook to the latest in cosmetic procedures. The authors first recommend a simple, common sense home regimen to help keep faces looking and feeling good: a healthy diet, well-cleansed skin, sufficient sleep and not too much exposure to the sun. The authors then discuss various skin problems along with treatments available. Although Brandt features the sometimes controversial Botox method, he also covers the many alternatives that may be helpful (chemical peels, microdermabrasion, laser surgery) as well as over-the-counter products (moisturizers and creams). Brandt helps demystify the many quick and painless solutions to wrinkles, crow's feet and other age-related problems and help readers assess how much money to spend and which products and treatments are worth it. When considering any medical treatment, the authors stress finding a competent, experienced professional to increase chances for success.

Using Botulinum Toxins Cosmetically: A Practical Guide

By Jean Carruthers, Alastair Carruthers

Provides the practical, clinical aspects of the cosmetic use of botulinum toxins. Discusses the problems and possibilities of this type of treatment and discusses the aesthetic philosophy, brow injections, horizontal forehead lines, per orbital area, mid and lower face, and cervical injections. CD-ROM contains commentary on the techniques described in text.

Book Description

The two pioneers in the cosmetic use of botulinum toxins (such as BOTOX®) have here produced an easy-to-read highly illustrated guide for those wishing to know about the practical clinical aspects of the treatments. Their backgrounds in plastic surgery, dermatology and ophthalmology make the authors uniquely aware of all the possibilities offered and problems raised by this phenomenally popular modality. The integral CD-ROM includes over 40 minutes of filmed procedures with commentary.

Textbook of Facial Rejuvenation: The Minimally Invasive Combination Approach

By Nicholas J. Lowe

Book info

Southern California Dermatology, Laser and Psoriasis Center, Santa Monica. Provide details on the current treatments and combination of therapies for optimum results tailored for individual patients. Topics include photo protection, combination chemical peels, vascular lesions, YAG laser rejuvenation, and skin resurfacing. Colour photographs are included.

Client Intimacy

By Fred Wiersema

Mr Wiersema is a business strategist and author

The Discipline of Market Leaders

By Fred Wiersema

Face the Media

By Judith Byrne

"Whatever qualities the rich may have, they can be acquired by anyone with the tenacity to become rich. The key, I think, is confidence. Confidence and an unshakable belief it can be done, and that you are the one to do it".
Felix Dennis

1.4 Recommended Procedure Selection and Key Responsibilities

Most cosmetic practice falls into six broad categories as follows:

■   Freelance dentists, Nurses, Surgeons, Physicians and other specialities without practice structure

■   Dentists, Physicians and Surgeons with support staff including a RGN or Dental hygienist

■   Plastic surgeons with small support staff excluding a nurse (NHS Structure)

■   Plastic surgeon with nurse and support staff (Private)

■   Large cosmetic clinic

■   Private hospitals providing cosmetic treatments

The recommendations below provide solutions for most situations. In each example, I have recommended a model of how responsibilities and compensation can be structured. By choice, I have excluded a model for hospitals and large clinics. The examples provided can be modified to fit a clinic and hospital scenario.

Option 1- Freelance (Dentists-Nurses-Surgeons GP's-Other Specialties) with no support structure

Operating out of Salons, Spas, Gyms etc...

For simplicity, I will refer to all relationships with external businesses as "Business Associate". The Business Associate provides the support and marketing for a percentage of the clinician's profit. In most cases, the Business Associate will want a percentage of the gross revenue and in this case, I recommend that you negotiate wisely, regardless of the Business Associate's enthusiasm to generate an enormous amount of clients. Wait and see the result and leave room for further negotiations.

The percentage should be negotiated on a tier system based on the Business Associate's ability to market the services to its client base. You will never know how well the Business Associate will contribute to your business until the project begins and in most cases, the negotiation can be re-evaluated once you can assess the contribution of your Business Associate. In most cases, the clinician will have to work very hard to generate interest for his or her services so do not give away your soul in the beginning. If you require assistance in negotiation and starting up a salon led business you should purchase our Business in a Box CD, which provides examples of ways to negotiate with salons and spas. This CD will also provide training manuals and other resources which you will need to operate successfully in salons. Below is an example of how the responsibilities should be shared between the Salon Owner and the Clinician.

Procedures Selection & Key Responsibilities

Dermal fillers	Provided by clinician Average profit: £175/treatment Duration: initially 45 minutes
Radiesse™	Provided by clinician/nurse Average Profit: £400/£300/session Duration: 45mins/50mins/session
Botulinum Toxin	Provided by clinician Average profit: £150/treatment. Duration: 30 minutes
Facial peels	TCA and AHA Provided by clinician Average profit: varies Duration: 30 minutes
Skin Care	Provided by clinician. Discuss with Business Associate to ensure that there is no conflict of interest. It is best to split the profit 50/50 with the owner to prevent friction. Cosmeceuticals are more effective treatments for patients who need to repair damaged skin and assist with the ageing process and these products can only be sold by medical professionals.
Mesotherapy	Provided by clinician Average Profit: £70/£100/session Duration: 20mins/30mins
Sclerotherapy	Provided by Clinician Average Profit: £100/£120 session Duration: .5 hour session

Receptionist

Core responsibilities
Answer telephones
Schedule appointments
Follow-up on appointments
Greet cosmetic clients and provide medical histories and consent forms and other related information.

Secondary *responsibilities*
Work with clinician to market aesthetic services to the salon's client.

Remuneration
If the receptionist is enthusiastic, the salon owner and the clinician should include a bonus scheme to motivate this individual to market the medical aesthetic services

Training on telephone sales and Customer service
Provided by the clinician & manuals can be purchased from K-T Training Retail Division.

**Hairdressers
And Aestheticians**

Mainly work on commission so these individuals are not obligated to promote medical aesthetic services. It is the clinician's responsibility to educate the stylist and aesthetician on the benefits of his/her services.

The clinician needs to help the employees to understand that by promoting medical aesthetic services, they are providing a valuable service to their clients since enhancing one's beauty is an integrated approach.

Remuneration

Free treatment or a referral fee whichever is appropriate.

Clinician

Core Responsibilities
To provide treatments to patients
To work with Business Associate's staff to market service to clients

Remuneration
Profit after direct cost and commissions.

I hope it is apparent to all who plan to work with a Business Associate that the more procedures you offer the more profitable the clinic session will be since it is very difficult to fill up a clinic session with only botulinum toxin and dermal filler procedures. Most salons that provide non-surgical procedures are possibly providing the service via a remote service. This means that the freelance clinician runs schedule clinics on specific days and is not available locally. With this type of scenario, the clinician is only providing limited services which are convenient for the clinician to administer without a follow-up. If you provide more services than the present clinician, and you are local to the area, do not be fearful to convince the Business Associate that your skills and professionalism are superior to the present clinician, and that you will generate larger revenue and profit in each session. Do not ignore the local factor and ways it contributes to higher customer care resulting in higher customer satisfaction.

For more information on developing a "Business Associate" structure, contact us at info@kttraining.co.uk or purchase our **Business in a Box CD**.

Option 2 – Freelance (Dentists- Nurses- Physicians- Other Specialties) No Support Structure & No Office

Operating out of Salons, Spas, Gyms and your home etc...

For simplicity, I will refer to all relationship with external businesses as **"Business Associate"**.

In this case the Business Associate rents space to the independent clinician. Sometimes the rental will include telephone answering and scheduling services. However, there are no marketing commitments and client generation is the clinician's responsibility. Similarly, if the independent clinician wants to run a clinic from home, the marketing responsibilities are left to the clinician. Space rental and running the business from your home is a more profitable situation in the long run, but it is difficult to set up in the initial phase, and it will take much more capital investment in the beginning. In option 1, the Business

Associate provides the support (receptionists, clients, prime location, comfort, ambiance, coffee,) and marketing (business associate has access to new clients on a daily basis, has web site, has successful service oriented business targeting the correct demographic) for a percentage of the independent clinician's profit.

In Option 2, patient generation is going to be very difficult in the beginning until you are established and is known in the local market. This may take a year or longer depending on your free time. Most new clinicians working in the NHS system prefer option 1 with option 2 representing their intermediate plan and owning a clinic representing their long term plan. Most businesses operate similarly with short, medium and long term plans. The objective is to minimize financial risk and business start up time.

Procedures Selection & Key Responsibilities

Dermal fillers	Provided by clinician Average profit: £175/treatment Duration: initially, 45 minutes
Radiesse™	Provided by clinician/nurse Average Profit: £400/£300/session Duration: 45mins/50mins/session
Botulinum toxin	Provided by clinician Average profit: £150/treatment. Duration: 20 minutes
Facial peels	TCA and AHA Provided by clinician Average profit: varies Duration: 30 minutes
Skin Care	Recommendation Provided by clinician Average profit varies

Receptionist	**Core responsibilities**
	Answer telephones
	Schedule appointments
	Greet cosmetic clients and provide medical histories and consent forms and other related information. (Probably for a fee)
	Secondary responsibilities
	Work with clinician to market aesthetic services to the client.
Clinician	**Core Responsibilities**
	To provide treatments to patients and to market his/her services to the local community via internet marketing, seminars, lectures, newsletters.
	Remuneration
	Profit after direct cost and Business Owner's commission

If your situation is similar to option 2, you have assumed more responsibilities than the individuals in scenario 1 so it is best that you manage your finance shrewdly. You will require funds to finance your business start up cost so it is best that you start with the core procedures and use your finance wisely to get the business set up properly. You may need a receptionist to answer the phone since it is not advisable to let the calls go to answer service. As you increase your income, you can invest in your personal and business development. Many of our past trainees took this approach or combined the two options and have done exceptionally well. In fact, it might seem challenging but over time, the clinician will begin to enjoy the art of business and the incredible skill sets he/she has developed in addition to his/her technical skills

 These two options are temporary situations since it is rare that you can build a million dollar business based on optimum customer service when the business is not yours to control. However, these two options are best for new clinicians who want to test the waters before they jump in.

Dentists, Other Specialties – Minimal Administrative Support – Office Structure- No Nurse

This situation is most common among NHS dental practices, and physicians of any specialty with private practices. In this scenario, the business owner has decided to fusion medical aesthetics into his/her practice to maximize revenue opportunities and increase profit. The first misconception among both dentists and physicians is that the business will come to them once they have completed their technical training. In most cases, there is little consideration as to how the practice will generate clients.

Some physicians seem to believe that clients will just appear out of the woodworks like they did in the NHS system. Even successful private clinics will encounter problems attracting clients for non surgical medicine. The non-surgical industry is much more competitive than any other area of medicine. For example, plastic surgeons in the United Kingdom competing among each other have approximately 400 competitors, and as most of these surgeons are NHS Consultants, the number of real competitors might be approximately 100 or less. In non-surgical medicine, there are thousands of competitors and every one of these individuals is aggressively competing for the limited amount of private clients available.

The biggest challenge I have with this structure is the practice owner, who is also the treatment provider, usually wants to provide only those treatments that gross over a specific amount of profit/hour such as Botulinum Toxin treatments and Dermal Filler treatments. However, these treatments are available at salons, gyms, and by nurses. It is nearly impossible to create any success with this strategy. I have also noticed that dentists tend to evaluate procedures not on market appeal but on hourly profitability and convenience for him/her. Not a good approach if you plan to be successful in this arena. The practice owners have to get out of the mindset of providing services which are convenient for the practice and not for the client. This includes the procedures offering as well as other services such as opening hours and well trained staff members who understand customer service. Below is my recommendation on procedures and responsibilities.

Procedures Selection & Key Responsibilities

Dermal fillers	Provided by clinician Average profit: £175/treatment Duration: Duration: initially, 45 minutes
Botulinum Toxin	Provided by clinician Average profit: £150/treatment Duration: Duration: 30 minutes
Facial peels	TCA and AHA Provided by clinician Average profit: varies Duration: 5 minutes for clinician and 20 minutes of prep time which can be facilitated by support staff
Skin Care	Recommendation by clinician and supported by office staff
Mesotherapy	Provided by clinician Average Profit: £70/£100/session Duration: 20mins/30mins
Radiesse™	Provided by Clinician Average Profit: £400/300 session Duration: 45mins/50mins/session

Receptionist	***Core responsibilities*** Answer telephones Schedule appointments Greet patients and cosmetic clients and execute pre- consultation protocols Follow-up on both telephone and web enquiries ***Secondary responsibilities*** Work with the internal team to market services to cosmetic clients ***Remuneration*** Salary Individual bonus Team bonus
Support staff	***Core Responsibilities*** Will be determined by the office manager ***Secondary responsibilities*** Work with the office team to meet sales objectives ***Remuneration*** Salary Team bonus
Clinician	***Core responsibilities*** Seeing insured patients ***Secondary responsibilities*** Seeing cosmetic clients **Manage cosmetic practice**

Dentists & Private Practice Owners

If you do not want to hold an evening clinic or work on Saturdays, I would recommend that you book 1 day per week or fortnight to treat aesthetic clients. Do not try to fit aesthetic clients in between regular patients. On busy practice days, it is extremely difficult to give aesthetic clients the attention they require from you and your staff. Aesthetic clients do not want to be rushed, and sometimes a consultation combined with a treatment can take up to 40 minutes or even an hour. If you have other patients waiting, and you are stressed for time you will not be able to give your aesthetic clients the attention they need. Furthermore, your support staff will feel pressured from waiting patients creating a tense environment. If you want to be successful in this area of medicine, you need to carefully plan your entry strategy.

Dentists, Other Specialties – Minimal Administrative Support – Office Structure - Nurse

This structure is similar to the structure above except the clinician has a nurse present who is qualified to administer almost all of the recommended procedures. This is an ideal situation since the clinician can delegate most of the labour intensive procedures to the nurse. However, the nurse must be suitable for the job. In my experience, a clinic owner who is providing the treatments to the clients usually achieves success quicker since the clinician has a stake in the success of the business.

Many nurses tend to lag behind because of poor selling skills and the lack of incentive to sell multiple procedures in one consultation. It is my observation that most nurses working for a basic salary will sometimes perform poorly due to lack of an incentive and poor training in customer service and sales. For instance, if your nurse does not care for aesthetic procedures and is agreeing to provide aesthetic treatments because you have asked her/him to do so, it is better to provide the procedures yourself. The profit from some procedures is not as high as others but these clients will possibly go on to being clients for other services that generate greater profit. In the United Kingdom and North America, there are many freelance nurse injectors who are prepared to work on an hourly basis to provide non-surgical treatments in a practice. If you feel you need a freelance nurse to assist you in your practice development, contact us at info@kttraining.co.uk.

Dentists

It is not yet established if dental hygienists can provide non surgical treatments and many manufacturers do not want their products being used by unqualified individuals, so it may be a bit difficult to leverage your time by delegating some of the responsibilities to someone in your practice who is not an RGN. However, there is nothing stopping you from hiring a contract RGN to facilitate some of the treatments which you may consider low return for your time. It is best to delegate even your favourite procedures such as Botox and Fillers to the nurse if your plan is to schedule clients among NHS patients or even private dental patients. I have observed that dentists work quickly and process many patients in a day. In this business, it is important to be relaxed and give the clients as much time to communicate their needs to you.

You also have to spend a great amount of time to set realistic expectations for the client. This can take up to 40 minutes but the result is miraculous if the client bonds with you. The essence of a good consultation with a medical aesthetic client is the relationship. The client needs to have confidence that the clinician has the capability of making him/her look better and this cannot be done quickly.

The beauty of this business is that when a client enters your premises for any treatment and the service and treatment outcome is greater than what they expected, there is a 90% guarantee that they will return for more services and this is the power of non-surgical medicine. They return because they like you and not because of need for your services. If you are planning to be successful in non-surgical medicine, you need to plan your strategy before you begin. Many of our clients are top dentists with very successful private practices, and they still feel the need to work with our consulting division to guarantee that their entire organization, including themselves, understands the importance of customer relationship in a private and competitive market. Please view (www.thebeautysociety.co.uk and www.rejuvadent.co.uk) to get a feel for the future of dentistry and facial aesthetics.

The procedure selection and key responsibilities are listed on the next page.

Procedures Selection & Key Responsibilities

Dermal fillers	Provided by clinician/nurse Average profit: £175/treatment Duration: initially, 45 minutes
Botulinum Toxin	Provided by clinician/nurse Average profit: £150/treatment. Duration: 30 minutes
Facial peels	Provided by clinician/nurses Average profit: varies Duration: 5 minutes for clinician and 20 minutes of prep time which can be facilitated by support staff
Skin Care	Recommendation by clinician/nurse and supported by office staff
Mesotherapy	Provided by nurse Average Profit: £70/£100/session Duration: 20mins/30mins
Radiesse™	Provided by clinician/nurse Average Profit: £400/£300/session Duration: 45mins/50mins/session
Consultation	Needs time and patience since you are trying to sell yourself and the practice's entire range of services so delegate to whoever can execute the best which in most cases is a person with sales skill.

Receptionist	***Core responsibilities*** Answer telephones Schedule appointments Greet patients and cosmetic clients and execute pre- consultation protocols Follow-up on both telephone and web enquiries ***Secondary responsibilities*** Work with the internal team to market services to cosmetic clients ***Remuneration*** Salary Individual bonus Team bonus
Support staff	***Core Responsibilities*** Will be determined by the office manager ***Secondary responsibilities*** Work with the office team to meet sales objectives ***Remuneration*** Salary Team bonus
Nurse Injector	***Core Responsibilities*** Consultation and delegated treatments ***Secondary responsibilities*** Work with the office team to meet sales objectives ***Remuneration*** Hourly salary/ commission only/or both
Clinician	***Core responsibilities*** Seeing present patient base ***Secondary responsibilities*** Seeing some cosmetic patients **Manage facial aesthetic division**

Plastic surgeons – NHS Consultants with private practices

Plastic surgeons have such a great opportunity to excel in non-surgical medicine since surgeons are better skilled at assessing the client's needs for overall improvement. However, some surgeons still feel that surgical procedures are more effective in achieving optimum results. The problem with this mindset is that most clients are not ready to make the difficult decision to undergo surgery and prefer to use a less invasive solution in the interim. If the client trusts the surgeon, he/she may move up to a surgical solution but this may take a year or two. In the mean time the surgeon should accept the client's decision until the client is prepared to undergo surgery.

The biggest challenge in the enhancement industry is every sector tends to be one-dimensional in scope-non-surgical clinicians tend to consider only non surgical solutions for their client's facial enhancement needs even if the client may require cosmetic surgery to achieve optimum results. On the other hand, surgeons tend to focus on surgical solutions to achieve optimum results without considering non-surgical alternatives. There needs to be integration of the two areas of cosmetic medicine.

Surgeons working as NHS consultants have a great advantage, since they are on the register and receive a large volume of referrals from GPs in the local area. I have observed that this is the most overlooked area for lead generation. Surgeons seem to be prepared to purchase referrals rather than develop this free referral base which is given to them. The most efficient means of generating free referrals is to develop well defined marketing material such as individual brochures on non-surgical and surgical procedures. You may need the help of a company such as K-T Solutions to advise you on your promotional mix. Once your promotional material has been developed, hire a part-time individual with sales ability to visit the individual doctor surgeries in the local area to promote your services. This individual can visit nearby salons and spas as well. There are benefits to being a surgeon, take advantage of them.

Things may have changed since I last worked with an NHS Consultant, but in my experience, every surgeon has an NHS secretary which most surgeons use to deal with their private clients as well. This situation is fine if the secretary is aware that private surgical and non-surgical clients need to be treated differently. The clients are paying for the surgeon's time, so they expect service. The preferred situation would be to hire a different person to manage your private clients. The surgeon may want to discuss his/her business model with a business consultant such as K-T Solutions to identify the appropriate business strategy for his/her long term success.

Below are my recommendations on procedure selection and key responsibilities. I will only discuss non-surgical options. The popular surgical procedures were identified in Section 1.1.

Procedures Selection & Key Responsibilities

Dermal fillers	Should be delegated to a freelance nurse
Botulinum toxin	Should be delegated to freelance nurse This treatment is very popular and in most situations this is where the nurse can bond with the client and sell multiple procedure such as fillers, peels, Radiesse and surgical procedures.
Facial peels	TCA can be administered by the surgeon and AHA procedure should be delegated to freelance nurse or both procedures can be provided by the nurse.
Sclerotherapy	Should be administered by the nurse
Radiesse™	This procedure can be done by the nurse but the mapping of the face can be executed by the surgeon since it is his/her expertise.
Mesotherapy	Treatment should be done by the nurse Peels and Mesotherapy are great treatments for any facelift patients so the surgeon should strongly recommend the treatment pre and post facelift.
Skin care	Recommendations by surgeon and supported by office staff and freelance nurse
Cosmetic surgery	Procedures provided by the surgeon

Secretary

Core responsibilities
Respond to web enquiries
Answer telephone and sell cosmetic services
to clients
Schedule appointments
Greet patients/clients
Remuneration
Salary
Individual bonus for managing cosmetic
clients

Free -Lance Nurse

Core responsibilities
Provide all non-surgical treatments
Provide all consultation for non-surgical
procedures
Can execute pre-consultation protocol for
plastic surgery procedures

Remuneration

Percentage of gross margin or hourly wage
with a small percentage of net profit
(just non surgical procedures)

Surgeon

Core responsibilities
Attending to NHS responsibilities
Secondary responsibilities
Consulting with cosmetic clients and
providing the treatments to clients.
**Manage cosmetic practice (very
important)**

There are more clients wanting non-surgical procedures than surgical procedures and there is a 50% chance that non-surgical clients will go on to become surgical clients. The 5 year value of one 25-year-old non-surgical client to a plastic surgeon's practice can look like this:

	Treatments	Revenue to practice
Year 1	Chemical Peels	£500
	Skin Care	£600
	Botulinum Toxin	£600
Year 2	Mesotherapy	£300
	Chemical Peels	£1100
	Skin Care	
	Botulinum Toxin	£600
	Dermal Filler	£400
Year 3	Skin Care and Chemical Peels	£1100
	Botox	£600
	Dermal Filler	£400
Year 4	Chemical Peels	£1100
	Skin Care	
	Breast Augmentation	£4,300
Year 5	Chemical Peels	£1100
	Skin Care	
	Others	£1000
Total Revenue		**£13,600**

This is the point that most surgeons fail to see. Non-surgical clients spend smaller increments of money per visit but over a five-year period, their contribution to the practice's revenue will surpass that of a one-time surgical client. There are also more clients wanting non-surgical services so why turn away clients who are so valuable to the long-term existence of the practice? Also, younger clients tend to be less conservative and are more open to speaking about their treatment, resulting in more referrals. Additionally, younger clients will stay a long time with their surgeons and will contribute higher annual revenue to the practice as they age.

Plastic surgeons in private practice

Procedures Selection & Key Responsibilities

Dermal fillers	Can be delegated to the appropriate staff nurse
Botulinum toxin	Should be delegated to the nurse once the client has been seen by the surgeon
Facial peels	TCA can be done by surgeon and AHA treatments can be delegated to staff nurse
Laser hair removal	Delegated to nurse or support staff
Microdermabrasion	Can be delegated to nurse or support staff
IPL	Can be delegated to the nurses
Skin care	Recommendations by surgeon and supported by office staff and freelance nurse
Radiesse™	Facial Mapping can be done by Surgeon and treatment can be provided by cosmetic nurse
	Supported by office staff
Cosmetic surgery	Surgeon

Receptionist

Core responsibilities
Respond to web enquiries
Responsible for marketing cosmetic procedure to Patients
Schedule appointments
Greet clients and execute pre-consultation protocol
Secondary responsibilities
Work with internal team to market cosmetic services to clients
Remuneration
Salary
Individual Bonus
Team Bonus

Nursing staff

Core responsibilities
Assist the surgeon
Administer some cosmetic treatments
Secondary responsibilities
Pre- and post-treatment care
Consultations with cosmetic clients (only if trained in customer service and sales)
Remuneration
Salary
Individual bonus
Team bonus

Support staff

Core responsibilities
Will be determined by the office manager
Secondary responsibilities
Work with the office team to meet sales objectives
Remuneration
Salary
Team bonus

Surgeon

Core responsibilities
Seeing cosmetic clients
Secondary responsibilities

Manage cosmetic practice with the help of a trained aesthetic practice manager or seek the assistance of a professional practice management consultant firm like K-T Solutions.

If you employ a nurse, the model for procedure offering and job responsibilities is the same as the previous example except your nurse will be paid a salary and her core responsibilities will involve more activities. However, if this individual is unsuitable for the position look elsewhere. I have repeated this statement a few times, but I will say it again. Private customers choose their surgeons and non-surgical specialists not just on expertise. Private clients are looking forward to developing a relationship with their cosmetic specialists so communication skills, appearance, personality and a number of other factors will play a part in the client's decision making process.

1.5 Setting Financial Objectives

Objectives set out what the practice is trying to achieve. Objectives can be set at two levels:

Practice level: These are objectives that concern the practice as a whole. For example, a practice objective might be:
To increase sales by 10% over the previous year-(top line sales objective).

To increase customer retention by 10% over a 2 year period- (customer retention objective)

To increase average customer spending by 20% over a two year period - (top line objective).

Functional level: In other words, specific objectives for each business unit. The cumulative result of each business unit's financial objective(s) should link up with the overall practice objectives.
For example, if one of your practice's financial objectives is to increase sales by 10% (which might translate into an increase in revenue of £100,000 from the previous year), then the combined increase in sales revenue of each business unit must equate to £100,000. If it does not, you need to make adjustments in either your practice's top-line objective or your functional unit top-line objective.

Both practice and functional objectives should follow the SMART criteria:

Specific: The objective should state exactly what is to be achieved.

Measurable: The objective should be measurable. You need to be able to evaluate your performance against the set objective.

Achievable: The objective should be realistic given the circumstances in which it is set and the resources available to the business.

Relevant: Objectives should be relevant to the people responsible for achieving them.

Time bound: Objectives should be set with a time frame in mind. The deadline should be realistic.

The following examples demonstrate how to set revenue objectives for some of the most popular business units.

 It is nearly impossible to manage a commercial business without planning how the business intends to achieve its financial objectives within a time period. Certainly, in my career, I have not worked for any company that did not have a thorough financial forecast and marketing plan for its upcoming year. Therefore, I am in awe that most medical practices do not prepare a financial and marketing plan for their upcoming year. There are possible two reasons for this behaviour: 1) traditional medicine operates as a monopoly and therefore, the business is guaranteed as much patients as it is prepared to take. This situation makes the planning process simple since the annual financial forecast is determined by calculating daily revenue times the amount of days in the year that the clinic is open. Very little forecasting skill is required in a situation such as this and there is no need for a marketing plan since the clinic does not need to make any effort to attract patients into its practice 2) medical professionals do not understand the need to plan and do not know how to plan.

However, in private practice, every business, including medical practices, needs to plan how the business intend to achieve its financial objectives. The financial plan is always supported by a thorough marketing plan. The marketing plan is the detail plan of how the business intends to drive clients through its doors. The marketing plan must be followed by a marketing budget. The marketing budget is a detail report on how much the business will spend to achieve its financial objectives for the year or period.

Example of first quarter financial forecast for an independent clinician.

Case Study 2

Procedure	Jan	Feb	March	Total
Botulinum Toxin	5	5	5	15
Revenue £250/treatment	£1250	£1250	£1250	£3750
Direct Cost 40 units at £1.4/unit	£280	£280	£280	£840
Gross Margin	**£970**	**£970**	**£970**	**£2910**
Dermal Filler	5	5	5	15
Revenue £275/syringe	£1375	£1375	£1375	£4125
Direct Cost £75/syringe	£375	£375	£375	£1125
Gross Margin	**£1000**	**£1000**	**£1000**	**£3000**
AHA Peels	6	6	6	18
Revenue £60/peel	£360	£360	£360	£1080
Direct Cost £5/peel	£15	£15	£15	£45
Gross Margin	**£345**	**£345**	**£345**	**£1035**
TCA Peels	3	3	3	9
Revenue £599/peel course	£1797	£1797	£1797	£5391
Direct Cost £89/peel course	£267	£267	£267	£801
Gross Margin	**£1530**	**£1530**	**£1530**	**£4590**
Skin Care	4	4	4	12
Revenue £100/sale	£400	£400	£400	£1200
Direct Cost 50% of revenue	£200	£200	£200	£600
Gross Margin	**£200**	**£200**	**£200**	**£600**
Gross Margin/month	**£5375**	**£5375**	**£5375**	**£16,125**

Let's look at how many hours in a month it will take the clinician to earn £5,375/month gross.

The clinician only needs to treat 19 clients and sell 4 skin care take home packages in a month to earn this type of gross margin. The clinician is providing treatments to approximately 5 clients a week and is selling one skin care home package in a week.

Clinic Session

Sessions	Monday	Tuesday	Wednesday	Thursday	Friday
½ hr. session	Consultation			AHA	
½ hr. session	Consultation			TCA	
½ hr. session	Consultation			Dermal Filler	
½ hr. session	Consultation			Botulinum Toxin	
½ hr. session	Consultation			Botulinum Toxin	
½ hr. session					
½ hr. session					

To treat 5 clients and sell one skin care home package will take the clinician no more than 3 hours a week. However, the clinician will have to spend some time consulting for free so I will add 2 hours for consultation. Therefore, the maximum time spent to generate £5375/month is approximately 20 hours/month. The hourly revenue is approximately £269/hour including consultation time or £447/hour for time worked. This is not bad at all for a new business to earn with so little start-up investment. You are also generating this level of income for working less than one day a week. If anything, the financial plan is a great motivator for practice owners. With a plan, the business owner is focused and knows his/her objectives before the period begin. To achieve success, one has to be prepared.

 The practice objective for this business model is £5,375/month for the first quarter.

The functional objectives are the procedure's gross margins/month which should total £5,375.

Dermal Filler Projection- Year 1

	Jan	Feb	Mar	Apr	May	Jun	Jul	Aug	Sept	Oct	Nov	Dec
New Patients	5	5	5	5	5	5	5	5	5	5	5	5
Revenue from new patients (£275/treatment)												
	1375	1375	1375	1375	1375	1375	1375	1375	1375	1375	1375	1375
Revenue from returning patients (£)												
							1375	1375	1375	1375	1375	1375
Monthly total revenue for year 1 (£)												
	1375	1375	1375	1375	1375	1375	2750	2750	2750	2750	2750	2750
Total dermal filler revenue in Year 1 = £24,750												

Dermal Filler Projection- Year 2

	Jan	Feb	Mar	Apr	May	Jun	Jul	Aug	Sept	Oct	Nov	Dec
New Patients	5	5	5	5	5	5	5	5	5	5	5	5
Previous year Patients (two treatments annually)												
Jan-Jun	5	5	5	5	5	5	5	5	5	5	5	5
Jul-Aug	5	5	5	5	5	5	5	5	5	5	5	5
Present Year Patients												
Jan-Jun							5	5	5	5	5	5
Total	15	15	15	15	15	15	20	20	20	20	20	20
Total Year 2 Revenue = 210 treatments at £275/treatment = £57,750												

Dermal filler business unit has increased by 130% in year two. Year two financial results will rarely materialise if the treatment results are poor and the clinic operates inefficiently. If you approach this business haphazardly, you will most certainly miss out on the repeat factor. In business, we call this the lifetime value of a customer. It is essential that you maximize the lifetime value of each customer for your long term success. To achieve repeat business in a competitive market, the business has to be managed effectively.

Equally, Botulinum Toxin and Skin Care monthly revenue will also begin to double in months April to June, triple in months July to September and quadruple in months October to December. These clients will return every 3 months for repeat products and treatments.

It is rare to achieve 100% repeat business, but you should aim for at least 80% retention rate. Most clinicians believe their retention rate to be 90% or more but when past revenue is evaluated, the figures never match up to the clinician's impression of his/her business success and numbers never lie.

Why Is It Important To Set Practice & Functional Objectives?

■ The financial plan is like a road map. It gives the owner a clear vision of what needs to be achieved in a month, quarter, half year and year end. A business can achieve success without a plan, but I can guarantee you that the same business can achieve its objective quicker if the business owner took the time to plan all business activities in advance.

■ The plan allows the business owner to measure his/her performance to the plan throughout the period and to identify and quickly rectify low performance areas.

■ By breaking down the business's monthly revenue by procedures (functional objectives) one can clearly identify where the business is falling short.

■ The financial plan allows the business owner to react quickly to problems rather than wait until the end of year to identify that the business has not met its objectives and is failing. For example, if year 1 July's dermal filler total is equal to or lower than June's figures, I would want to know why the business did not double its revenue for Dermal Filler. It can only be three things: the marketing efforts did not work for July which is highly unlikely since it has worked for all previous months, no repeat business due to lack of follow-up, or clients are not satisfied with the results of the treatment. Whatever the reason, I would fix the problem immediately.

■ The financial plan helps the business owner to explain his/her vision for the business to his/her employees. The plan is the most effective tool in communicating to staff members their importance in the business success. For instance, if dermal filler revenue is down in July and the problem is due to the poor follow-up by staff members, I can use the financials to demonstrate how employees' inefficiencies can impact sales, profit, job security, and bonuses.

■ The plan helps business owners to set effective bonus schemes since the bonus is tied to monthly/quarterly financial results. When employees have a clear vision of what they need to do to assist in achieving the practice's objectives, they are more motivated to assist in its success.

■ Even successful medical practices should get into the habit of setting financial objectives before the period begins. If you fail to plan you are planning to fail.

1.6 Developing your Marketing Plan and Marketing Budget

What is marketing?

Marketing is about understanding customers and finding ways to provide products or services which customers' desire. This statement may seem simple, but it is not. For instance, if a customer wants to purchase a computer, they may choose the product for a number of reasons such as price, ease of use, services, reliability etc..... The objective of the marketer is to identify the product's target markets and to determine the unique sets of benefits each target market values.

Most effective marketing campaigns sell benefits not products to the consumer. Hence, MAC cosmetics do not sell eye-shadows or lipsticks - they sell choices, good value, extensive colour range, knowledgeable sales staff, and lots more. This company came in and knocked out some major competitors because it knew its customers' needs and delivered. Most non-surgical clinicians do not truly know their client's needs. If they did, the industry would have more integrated specialists in the field. Non-surgical clinicians seem to think that if they offer everything, they will be successful in attracting customers into their practice. This is not marketing. If it were this easy, every cosmetic clinic would be successful but few are, especially the ones that offer everything to everyone.

The entire book is dedicated to helping its reader understand how to market their business. Marketing is not an easy discipline, but if you put some effort in learning the principals, you will outperform your competitors. The more practice that you have as a marketer; you will become stronger in protecting your local market. New competitors will find it difficult to attract your present clients, even if they are bigger and richer.

To put things into context, you may find it helpful to often refer to the following diagram which summarises the key elements of marketing and their relationships:

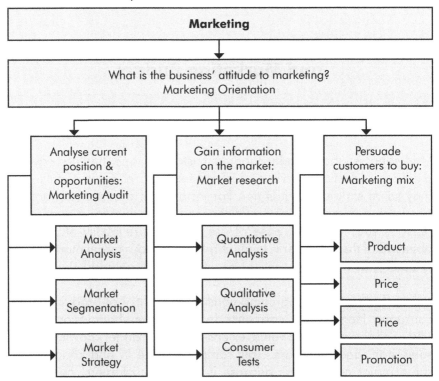

Market Analysis- The first section of chapter 1 went into detail about the largest medical aesthetic market (United States). I purposely introduced statistics to help you to understand what customers want based on the largest market in the world. When I came to Europe, many physicians and senior executives adamantly insisted that I did not know the European market and insisted that it is different from the United States. Seven years later, I see no difference in trends except that Europe and the United Kingdom are slower in adaptation, but eventually all popular treatments in the United States will become popular in the United Kingdom. What I have not seen is the reverse. Therefore, the United States statistics is the most reliable tool to use to conduct your marketing audit which we have done for you.

Market Segmentation- also covered in chapter one.

Marketing Strategy- Your strategy is a relationship strategy which focuses on developing a bond with your customers through superior treatment outcome, and added value services which are discussed throughout this book.

Quantitative Analysis, Qualitative analysis and Consumer Test- For small businesses as the one discussed in case study 2, these analyses are not needed. I think that any physician can achieve the figures that I have shown. However, if the business owner is planning to invest a large sum of money in new premises and capital equipment, I would recommend the analysis to establish if there is enough business in the local market to generate the projected revenue forecast needed to achieve breakeven point. Yet another reason for planning your business before you begin. The plan will identify hidden risks and can save you time and money. You may also attend our Business Course to learn how to plan and assess risks.

Marketing Mix or Persuading Customer to Buy- This component of marketing is detailed in the Marketing Plan. I expect the clinician to develop his/her own Marketing Plan. Below is a case study of how to develop your own plan.

Case Study 3

The marketing plan to support the financial plan discussed in case study 2 is fairly simple but planning is essential if you are going to meet your financial objectives.

New Businesses without a database of patients.

Your marketing activities should consist of the following activities:

■   Develop promotional material-(business cards, one corporate brochure, individual procedure brochure, gift certificates, appointment cards, and referral cards. (If you are trained by K-T Training, this information is given to you for free, but if you wish to purchase the scripts from us, this can be done by contacting our office at info@kttraining.co.uk).

■   You need to create a great logo which will appear on all of your communication messages.

■   You need a web site – the site needs to be stylishly designed. Chapter 5 discusses the key elements of a web site.

■   You need to run regular information seminars to attract the public into your premise on an informal basis.

■   You need to develop seminar presentation for the public. (Can be purchased from K-T Training Retail Division)

■   You need to develop interdependent relationships with gym, salons, hairdressers, and boutique owners. Identify businesses that presently market their services to your potential target markets. For instance, if you identified your target markets as the following: 19-30 age group, 31-45 age group and 45+ age group, you will have a better chance of reaching 19-30 target market in places such as gyms. The 31-45 (Middle class) age group can be targeted through boutiques. I hope it is becoming clear to you why it is important for you to understand target marketing. The different target groups may have the same desire for improving their appearance but each target group behaves differently and has different lifestyle choices. It is your job to know your target groups, know where to find them, and know how to communicate with them. I will discuss how to develop relationships with external businesses in Chapter 5 (Promotion)

Marketing Activities (Market Mix) & Marketing Budget

To open the business in January, I recommend developing the marketing plan in October of the previous year. Below is a simple guide line on how to develop a marketing plan. The plan should be done on a financial spreadsheet in Excel.

	Oct	Nov	Dec	Jan	Feb	Mar
Promotional Material	Concepts and scripts		Completed			
			£1500			
Seminars	Plan adverts and identify where to promote the seminar		Place ad for seminar or mail invitations to the database of one of your business relationships	1st		2nd
			£500	£500		£500
Seminar Presentations	Develop		Completed			
			£100/one time/cost			
Website Development	Begin		Completed			
			£1,000/one time cost			
Web Site Optimization and marketing				start		
				£100	£100	£100
Interdependant Relationships	Begin to develop					
			Possibly free treatment or a % deal			
Newsletters	Script and concept		Finish	Distribute		
			£300	£100		
Advertising in local magazines	Least attractive option					
				£400		
Total			£3,550	£1100	£100	£600

This marketing plan is much more aggressive than what is needed to generate the financial forecast discussed in case study 2. The planned activities should generate twice as much business.

Existing businesses with a customer base should include mailers to its present customers as its first marketing activity. Therefore, the marketing plan for an existing business is similar to case study 3 with mail-outs to its present customers as a first priority. A Pre-developed letter can be found in our **Business in a Box CD**.

The Importance of the Marketing Plan & Marketing Budget

■   The plan identifies the activities needed to generate revenue.

■   It provides you with a clear view of the activities that need to be accomplished and their timeline.

■   It identifies the financial resources required to support ongoing client generation.

■   The plan will minimize financial risks.

■   The plan will keep you and your staff focused on the practice's global objectives.

 Execution of the marketing plan does not guarantee that the financial objectives will materialize since the marketing plan's objective is to generate client interest for your services. A marketing plan can fail if the business's internal structure is inefficient. Telephone management, receptionist selling skills, improper scheduling, office hours, and poor consultation skills will slow down business success dramatically. Most private medical clinics, including dental practices, have experienced poor results from their marketing campaign due to inefficient internal structure. I have had many clients who expected me to make their business a success without implementing change within their internal structure. It is impossible to do, and I now choose my clients carefully. If you are working in a salon situation, the internal structure is what will make you lag behind, and it is why I suggested that you may want to own your own premises if you plan to be very successful since you need control over every aspect of the business.

Our Business in a Box CD provides comprehensive planning templates to assist in new business set up or to help existing businesses manage their future performance more effectively. For more information on this product, contact us at info@kttraining.co.uk

1.7 Choosing your Supplier

There are more than 30 different manufacturers of dermal fillers in the market, 25 different manufacturers of micro-dermabrasion equipment and an infinite number of skin care companies. Each one claims their products produce the best results and is backed by science. For new clinicians to choose a supplier in any procedure category can be frustrating and confusing. Clinicians cannot align themselves with every supplier and selecting your key supplier in each category can be difficult. Unfortunately, I cannot provide you with information on every manufacturer in each procedure category, so I have decided to provide you with information on the industry leaders in five key areas: dermal fillers/volumisers, skin care, bio stimulation, chemical peels, and botulinum toxins. I have homed in on these procedures because they are the most profitable non-surgical procedures to any practice, and if you are running an aesthetic practice, these procedures should definitely be a part of your procedure offering.

Please contact us at info@kttraining.co.uk if you have specific questions on a particular product, equipment, or manufacturer.

Some basic tips when evaluating your supplier in any of the product categories:

■ Determine the length of time the manufacturer's product has been in the industry.

■ What is their track record of success in the business?

■ Is the product CE or FDA approved?

■ Are there any clinical papers available on the product's efficacy?

■ Does the manufacturer provide ongoing support for its product?

■ What kind of marketing support is available to you?

■ Can the manufacturer supply you with names of customers who are presently using the product?

■ Is the supplier the manufacturer of the product or a distributor?

■ Delivery charges ?

■ Are the sale representatives resourceful, do they understand the business of aesthetic medicine, and can they provide added value service to yourself or the practice?

■ Does the manufacturer engage in any marketing strategy to drive customers into your practice?

I commonly categorize the hundreds of products available in the market into the following subgroups similar to the target marketing concept:

Topical Treatments: Topical treatments in medicine can be the following: cosmeceutical skin products, sun care products, Retin A etc... Topical treatments are treatments that the client administers by themselves at home. The clinician provides instructions on how to use the treatments to manage the client's anti-ageing needs. It goes without saying that you should have a range of topical treatments available for your clients. When someone chooses to have non-surgical treatments, the assumption is they care about their appearance. Therefore, non surgical clinicians should take it upon themselves to find out what the client presently uses for home care and the clinician should provide recommendations on ways the client can manage or assist in maintaining and improving his/her appearance on a daily basis.

Texturing Procedures: These procedures improve the quality of the skin. Texturing treatments are as follows: chemical peels, IPL treatments, laser resurfacing treatments and microdermabrasion treatments.

Volumising Procedures: These are procedures which build volume in the dermis. Volumizers can be: the entire range of fillers, Radiesse, and possibly Radio Frequency Treatments.

Muscle Relaxants: These are treatments that paralyze the muscle resulting in a more youthful appearance. The most popular muscle relaxant is of course Botox®; however, there are a few new competitors in the market.

Bio-stimulation Treatments: These are treatments that improve skin texture, hydration, skin laxity, and skin stimulation with an anti-ageing effect. Mesotherapy is a biostimulation procedure.

Surgical Procedures: most people would like to avoid any kind of surgery for as long as possible but if the individual has excessive skin laxity, jowls, drooping eyelids, and deep static lines, the best possible option might be a face lift. I believe that it is best to make this recommendation as the first solution and if the client refuses to consult with a surgeon, you can recommend a program of non-surgical treatments which will improve the individual's overall appearance.

In business when information is disorganised, ambiguous and chaotic, the **affinity chart or diagram** is used to begin to bring order out of chaos. The categorization of the treatments into sub category is my affinity diagram and looks like the chart below.

Affinity Diagram

	Topical	Texturing	Volumizers	Muscle Relaxants	Bio-Stimulation	Surgery
Dry Skin	Yes				Yes	
Sun-Damaged Skin	Yes	Yes			Yes	
Fine Lines		Yes	Yes			
Deep Wrinkles		Yes	Yes			
Scars			Maybe			
Hyperpigmentation	Yes	Yes				
Lines around eyes			Yes	Yes		
Forehead Lines				Yes		
Frown Lines				Yes		
Drooping mouth			Yes			
Thin Lips			Yes			
Jowls					Maybe	Yes
Double Chin					Maybe	Yes
Excessive Sagging Skin						Yes
Cellulite					Yes	
Localized Fat Deposits					Yes	Yes

If you are still undecided on what procedures to offer, the affinity diagram should help you out. My recommendation is to select one or two options in each category. I plan to discuss the best possible options for each category in the next section. This is a great diagram to have in your consultation room to educate the clients on the different treatments available. It is a great visual representation of why different treatments have to be combined to achieve the results that many clients expect. The more tools you have available to help the client understand the logic behind your recommendation, the quicker you will bond with the client.

Feel free to duplicate. My diagrams are usually more attractive than this one, and I laminate the diagrams if I use them as sales aid. The affinity diagram is also an effective training tool for your receptionists and administrative staff. I can assure you that your staff do not know the differences between the ranges of non surgical options you presently provide.

Skin Care (Topical Treatments) – Cosmetic Cosmeceuticals Products

Cosmetic skin care products only serve to cleanse and maintain the skin. In contrast to cosmetics, cosmeceuticals will alter the structure and function of the skin. They reverse sun damage, reduce the appearance of wrinkles, and treat acne. Below are some of the ingredients and science behind some of the most used ingredients found in cosmetic cosmeceuticals products.

When evaluating a manufacturer's product, investigate if the product range contains the following important ingredients. The skin care ranges that I recommended contain all of the ingredients that I have listed below. The products are moderately priced so that you can make a healthy margin and the end price to the consumer is competitive with ordinary cosmetic products found in Boots, pharmacies, and high street stores.

Popular Cosmeceuticals Ingredients

Vitamin E: helps to smooth the skin, prevents premature aging of the skin by blocking lipid per oxidation responsible for cell membrane damage in tissues. Vitamin E has anti-inflammatory properties, helps to inhibit erythema formation caused by UV radiation, and helps in wound healing. Products with vitamin E as an active ingredient is great for daily protection and reinforce the protective factor of the sun block.

Vitamin C or ascorbic acid: is a well-known water-soluble anti-oxidant coming from natural sources and fruit and vegetables. Vitamin C is known to be an essential co-factor for the formation and function of collagen. Products with Vitamin C are also great for daytime protection because Vitamin C is an anti-oxidant and protects the skin from damaging free radicals and harmful sun rays.

B5): vitamin B5 is present in all living cells and is a constituent of c0-enzyme A, which is necessary for the synthesis of lipids, proteins, and the linkage between lipids, proteins and carbohydrates. Deficiency of Vitamin B5 can result in many dermatological disorders.

Lactic acid (alpha hydroxy acid): is generally considered to be one of the most effective naturally occurring humectants in the skin. Lactic acid has also been shown to reduce excessive epidermal keratinisation in cases of hyperkeratosis. Lactic Acid is a polyhydroxy acid and products with this key ingredient can be used both day and night. Dehydrated skin can use this product in the night for hydration. If needed, the client can use a lactic acid product in the daytime as well; however, they will require protection so a sun block is needed. To protect the skin from free radicals and harmful sun rays, the clinician can also include an anti oxidant product such as Vitamin A and Vitamin C.

Hyaluronic acid: the most efficient water binder, water buffer and anti-oxidant. Dehydrated skin will benefit from products that contain hyaluronic acid. The skin will still need daily protection so the client will need a strong sun protector.

Squalane: oil naturally occurring in human skin and is an important functional part of the lipid system. Products with this active ingredient will treat dry skin and is used for night and day care. Sun protection is required in the day.

Canella Asiatica: a botanical agent, which increases collagen production by inducing its precursor enzyme. This ingredient has a shelf life of 6 months, which is why you will not find it in stores. This amazing material reduces the appearance of stretch marks and is currently being researched for its effects on varicose veins.

Salicyclic acid: a proven anti-bacterial destroying agent. Products with this active ingredient will benefit patients with acne. Non greasy sun protection is needed in the daytime.

Retinol: a vitamin A treatment, which accelerates the skin cells' natural exfoliation process and diminishes the appearance of fine lines and wrinkles. Products with Retin A can improve skin tone and skin imperfections since Retin A is an effective exfoliate. If the client is using an anti-oxidant cream in the day with a sun protector, a product with Retin A or Retinol can be used in the night time as an exfoliator. For mature clients you may want to include another nourishing night care which can be alternated with the use of Retin A for night care.

Glycolic acid: a natural fruit acid, which accelerates the skin's cellular turnover. It improves circulation and produces vibrant, smoother, younger-looking skin. Glycolic Acid products produce similar results to a Retin A product so either one can be used to help exfoliation of the skin. Products with Retin A and Glycolic Acid should be included in a client home care since exfoliation is necessary to keep the skin healthy and young looking.

DMAE: a natural substance that stabilizes and strengthens the cell's plasma membrane. Dramatically tightens, firms, and tones the neck, eyelids, and facial muscles, resulting in a lean, toned, and youthful look. The results are temporary but creams with DMAE are great for flaccid skin and can be used day and night. I prefer to recommend creams with this active ingredient as a day care since it does give a temporary lift to the face. Sun care is required if used in the daytime.

Sodium hyaluronate: a protein that functions as a lubricant between the connective tissues of the skin, allowing the retention of skin's natural moisture, leaving the skin soft, supple and silky smooth. Other ingredients include Dimethicone Copolyol Meadowfomate, which is an anti-irritant, retinyl palminate, an anti-wrinkles agent, and actifirm, a skin-firming agent.

How do you select your product lines?

Every decision I make in business is based on the client's needs and satisfaction. Customers' needs differ based on their age and skin damage. Eighty percent of customers are also price sensitive so you will have to choose a few lines as follows: low end line, medium end line and possibly a high end line. You can mix and match between lines regardless of what the manufacturer's representative will advise you. Most Dermatologists use multiple products from different lines to meet the client's needs. To simplify things I will demonstrate how I make decisions utilizing the Affinity Diagram.

Affinity Diagram for Skin Care

Target Group	Problems	Patient Profile	Needs	Benefit
18-25 age group	Poor skin texture Acne/Blemishes	Quick Results Price Sensitive	AHA to exfoliate Salicylic acid for acne	Salicylic Acid and AHA will control oil and improve acne prone skin while improving skin texture.
25-35 age group	Poor skin texture- Hyper- pigmentation- Sun damage skin- Ageing skin	Price Sensitive with a budget- Quick Results- Convenience	AHA to improve skin quality. Kojic Acid for hyperpigmentation. Vitamins A, C, E, for protection against sun damage.	AHA-Younger appearance Improved Skin Quality- A, C, E-Protection and Anti-Ageing- Kojic Acid-Evenness of skin tone and reduction of melanin activity.
35-45 age group	Skin laxity- Hypepigmentation- Fine lines- Sun damage- Poor skin texture	Higher income but still price sensitive- Results- Convenience- One stop facility	AHA to exfoliate and improve skin texture- Kojic Acid for hyperpigmentation- Vitamins A, C, E, for ageing and sun damage- DMAE for skin laxity	Same as above DMAE is a natural substance that stabilizes and strengthens the cell's plasma membrane.
45-55 age group	Same as above but to a greater degree	Results- Convenience- One stop facility- Value for money but not as price sensitive as the above target group	Same as above.	This age range needs are similar to the above target group but there may be more damage to the skin so you may have to combine non-surgical and surgical treatments with skin care to make dramatic inroads.
55+	Same as above with excessive skin laxity resulting in sagging skin and redistribution of fat in the lower face	Results- Price Sensitive	Same as above but plastic surgery may be necessary to improve facial appearance	Same as above but plastic surgery may be necessary to improve facial appearance

Selling skin care products to the public requires training. The training is not in the product line but in diagnosing the client's skin condition and understanding how certain ingredients found in Cosmeceutical products can improve the client's skin.

Cosmeceutical skin care cannot prevent ageing but the principal ingredients found in the products will help to slow down and improve certain skin conditions associated with ageing. For instance, kojic acid is a melanin suppressor. By applying a cream with kojic acid as its active ingredient, the patient will benefit from a clearer and more even complexion. Hyperpigmentation is a common problem among ageing skin. Dryness and skin flaccidity is also a common problem with ageing skin so you will need products with hyaluronic acid or DHEA as its active ingredients to help this type of skin condition.

It is best to attend our cosmetic dermatology and skin care course to develop expertise in this area. For more information e-mail us at info@kttraining.co.uk

Below are the names of some reputable cosmeceutical manufacturers. Some of the manufacturers also make AHA Peels and TCA Peels and this information is highlighted in the chart. The next section discusses the advantages of peel procedures.

Skin Care Manufacturers

Product	Manufacturer Information	About the Company	Key Hydroxy	Alpha Hydroxy	TCA
			Present	Peels	
Skin Ceuticals (high end line)	Customer Sales line- 020 8997 8541 Sales: sales@skinceuticals.co.uk	Great product line and I strongly recommend that you include the CE Furolic, B Hydrater and Glycolic wash as part of your offering.	Yes	Yes	No
Skin Tech Medium end line)	Euromedical Systems Ltd is the UK Distributor Telephone and Fax numbers :0845 130 4949 International : + 44(0)1949838111	This is a medical line which is attractively priced. It allows the physician to sell a great product and make excellent margins.	Yes	Yes	Yes
Neostrata Low End Line.	Wigmore Medical +44(0) 207 491 0150	I love this line because it is effective and very inexpensive for the client. The company only trains medical professionals which is another benefit.	Yes	Yes	Not in the UK
Mene and Moy	Distributed by Medical Aesthetic Group	I have not worked with the line but the feed back is positive and the line also includes a TCA option which is convenient.	Yes	Yes	Yes

Chemical Peels

With the public's increasing interest in rejuvenation of the skin and slowing down the aging process, chemical peeling has emerged as a supplement to a total skin care program and most reputable manufacturers of chemical peels also manufacture a complete range of skin care products to complement the treatment.

Alpha Hydroxy Acids Peels

What are alpha hydroxy acids?

This group of naturally occurring acids is found in certain plants and fruits, including apples, grapes, citrus and sugar cane. Alpha hydroxy acid products have been used for hundreds of years as moisturizers and freshening agents, and over the last ten years the use of these

117

agents has expanded to include the treatment for acne, weathered-sun-damaged skin, pigmented skin, and fine wrinkles.

How do alpha hydroxy acids improve the appearance of the skin?

In all people, a thick layer of dead skin cells covers the surface of the skin and gives the complexion a rough, dull appearance. AHAs (alpha hydroxy acids), when used regularly, act as exfoliants, which lift away these dead skin cells and give the skin a healthier, rejuvenated appearance. Continued use of alpha hydroxy acids appear to stimulate new cell growth, which over time can make the skin appear more youthful and can encourage tightening of the skin, which becomes lax with age.

Can alpha hydroxy acids only be applied in physicians' offices?

There are many products which contain alpha hydroxy acids that are marketed for home use, including cleansers, astringents, creams, lotions, gels and sunscreens. These products can be used as a regular part of a home hygiene routine. Alpha hydroxy acid peels are a more concentrated solution that can only be applied in the clinician's office by specially trained staff. The solution is applied to the skin and left in place for a specified period of time depending on the client's skin type, and then neutralized, or washed off. This causes the upper layers of the skin in the treated areas to peel away over a period of several days. These peels are usually very light and do not require patients to miss any time from regular activities. However, because they are very light peels, several treatments may be required to achieve the desired results.

Can anyone use alpha hydroxy acids?

Because they are a naturally occurring product, alpha hydroxy acids have been determined to be safe for use by most people.

Are all alpha hydroxy peels the same?

No, the PH of the acid, bioavailability of free acid, and the concentration of the acid will determine the effectiveness of the peel. I have observed that companies, who claim to be cosmeceutical companies but sell peel solutions to aesthetician or beauty specialists do not create peels that are as effective as the medical grade peels. Clinicians believe that the strength of the peel is what matters, but this is not the case. A high concentration peel with a high PH will be less effective than a similar peel with a lower PH. The acidity of the peel is an important factor in the effectiveness of the peel. Neostrata's lowest strength peel has a PH of 1.6 which makes its lowest strength peel more effective than some 70% peels with PH of 3.6 or more.

 Do not choose your chemical peel course based on price of the course. Ask what type of peels you will be training with and investigate the product before you take the course. Many clinics are providing inferior quality peels and charging high prices, resulting in customer dissatisfaction and little repeat business. In any type of business including medical aesthetics, over-delivering on treatment results is the surest way to strengthen your long term success. Knowing the products that deliver excellent results is important to make the business a success.

You may want to attend our business courses if you need help in this area.

TCA Peels

What are TCA peels?

TCA (trichloroacetic acid) is a chemical applied only in a clinician's office to create a slightly deeper peeling effect than alpha hydroxy acids. TCA peels can effectively improve many conditions, including weathered skin, freckling, pigmentation, sun damage, fine wrinkles, and shallow acne scars.

How is a TCA peel performed and what happens to the skin following the peel?

TCA is applied to the skin and timed very carefully, the purpose being to induce a frosted appearance to the skin. The solution is

119

then neutralized, or washed off. Most patients experience a burning sensation while the solution takes effect. The peel causes the upper layers of skin cells to dry up and peel off over a period of days, exposing a new layer of healthier skin.

How much recovery time is required with a TCA peel?

While recovery times vary with the individual, most people require approximately 8-10 days to heal from an average TCA peel. The skin appears sunburned and will require some care at home. No time off work is required but there is some minor inconvenience such as excessive exfoliation.

 Anyone taking a peel course should choose a course that teaches both TCA and AHA, or you should take individual peel courses side by side. Except for the young, most individuals in their 30's or 40's need improvement to their skin and will require the TCA peel, however, many of your clients might not want to choose the TCA option due to financial constraints and inconvenience. In situations such as this one, it is best not to send the client elsewhere but to provide the simpler solution even if it is not the most appropriate solution. You need training on both procedures to achieve optimum results for your clients. K-T Training is the only company to provide a combined course on both peels. We also lecture on the ICP peel which is sensational for ethnic skin.

Dermal Fillers Review

There are three categories of dermal fillers in the industry.

Bio-degradable products. These are non-permanent products that will breakdown over a certain period of time. The average duration of the product will depend on the individual and the areas treated. Bio-degradable products have improved in persistence since the days of collagen and today the average treatment will last for up to 6-8 months. Therefore, most individuals can afford the treatment, and it is not necessary that physicians experiment with permanent products which are associated with severe adverse events.

Semi-permanent products: These products are usually longer lasting than the biodegradable products. Therefore, they are useful when the clinician wants to volumize large areas such as the cheek bones and lower face. In situations like these, bio-degradable products can be used but the amount of product needed to volumize a large area of the face can amount to 5 ml or more of product making the treatment cost prohibitive for the average client. In situations like these, semi-permanent products are used since the cost is less for the client over the long term. My favourite product in this category is Radiesse™ because of its long lasting and predictable characteristics. The most recent US statistics indicate that this product acceptance in the US is growing dramatically.

Permanent products: Some cosmetic clinicians may use permanent products with success, but in my experience these products are associated with severe adverse events. I cannot mention the name of the product that Leslie Ash was treated with but the product is a permanent product and is still being used today. I do not feel that the usage of permanent products is necessary since the client's face will change as he/she ages and the treatment result may not suit his/her face over time. Lips, for one, should not be treated with permanent fillers.

Below is a review of some of the most popular dermal filler products in the market. I have my favourites and if you need advice on how to select dermal fillers, contact us at info@kttraining.co.uk

Dermal Fillers Products and Manufacturer Information

Bio Degradable Products

Restylane – Perlane - Restylane Fine Line

The first Hyaluronic product to be developed and is still a market leader.

Active ingredients	HA 20mg/ml non-animal, stabilized Hylauronic acid
Volume:	1.0 ml Perlane 1.0 ml Restylane 0.4 ml Restylane Fine Line
Persistence:	Market experience-approximately 6-9 months
Appearance	A viscous, transparent solution
Pre-Test Required:	No
Manufacturer:	Q-Med AB, Seminariegatan 21, SE-752 28 Uppsala, Sweden. Phone +46 18 474 90 00 Fax +46 18 474 90 01

Juvederm / Hydrafill

These products are manufactured and distributed by Allergan Corp. The products have been in the market for some time and have shown dramatic improvement since its approval. Juvederm/Hydrafill brand is a strong competitor to Restylane and Perlane.

Active ingredients	Hyaluronic acid (cross-linked)
Volume	Syringes of 0.55 ml and 0.8ml
Indications	Juvederm Ultra 2: fine wrinkles and facial lines Juvederm Ultra 3/Hydrafill Softline: medium dept lines such as nasolabial lines. Juvederm Ultra 4/Hydrafill Softline Max : deep lines and lip augmentation
Persistence	6- 8 months
Appearance	Viscoelastic transparent gel
Storage	2-25 degrees Celsius
Origin	Non –animal
Pre-test required	No
Manufacturer	*Corneal Laboratory, 31, rue des Colonnes du Trone, 75012 Paris, France

Bolotero

Belotero is a mono-phasic non-particulate hyaluronic acid gel manufactured as a poly-densifed matrix which provides support in dermal spaces, whilst avoiding clumping and lump formation. This smooth cohesive gel moves with even pressure through the needle, therefore reducing the incidence of bruising or swelling during treatment. The soft feel of the product once implanted gives a natural transition between treated and untreated areas. Belotero Basic and Soft have been available in the UK since 2007 with the greater density product 'Intense' being launched in February 2009.

Active ingredients	Hyaluronic acid (cross-linked)
Volume	Pre-filled Syringes of 1 ml
Indications	Belotero Soft for superficial lines and fine skin areas such as crows feet and décolletage.
	Belotero Basic for fine lines lines such as peri-oral and cheeks and for lip definition. Belotero Intense for deeper lines such as nasolabial folds and for lip and cheek enhancement
Persistence	6- 8 months
Appearance	Viscoelastic transparent gel
Storage	2-30 degrees Celsius
Origin	Non –animal
Pre-test required	No
Distributor	Merz Aesthetics, a division of Merz Pharma UK Ltd, 260 Centennial Park, Elstree Hill South, Esltree. WD6 3SR

Zyderm 1, Zyderm 11 and Zyplast

Patients need to be skin tested before treatment. Accepted in the US. However, hyaluronic acid based dermal fillers such as Restylane and Perlane have made impressive inroads in the US market since their approval in 2004. Refer to chapter one for information on market acceptance.

Active ingredients: Bovine dermal collagen from controlled herds

Volume: Zyderm1 and Zyplast: 35 mg/ml of solution
Zyderm11: 65mg/ml

Origin   Bovine Dermal Collagen

Persistence: 3 to 4 months

Indications: Zyderm 1: fine wrinkles and facial lines
Zyderm 11: forehead wrinkles, glabellar, mild or moderate nasolabial folds and wrinkles of the cheek, increase volume in lips.
Zyplast: deep lines and lip augmentation

Pre-Test Required: Yes-28 days observation period

Manufacturer: Inamed Aesthetics/Allergan
(North America) 5540 Ekwill Street, Santa Barbara, California, USA 93111

Tel: 805.683.676, fax: 805.967.5839
(International) Kilbride Industrial Estates Arklow, County Wicklow,
Ireland Tel: (+35) 340

Semi – Permanent Fillers

Radiesse™

This is an excellent product for treating large defects such as hollows in the cheeks, reshaping the chin and jaw line, and increasing tissue volume of the face. The product is flexible enough to be used in areas such as the nasolabials for longer lasting results. Over 50% of all facelift procedures were to the 55+ age group. Clearly, the 38-55 target market is postponing surgical facelift procedures for the future. However, this does not mean that the 38-55 target market lacks the desire to look younger. Radiesse is an excellent non-surgical option for facial sculpting and is an ideal treatment for the 38-55 target market. The advantage of this product over Sculptra™ is its ease of use and immediate results giving the clinician more flexibility with the treatment outcome. This product is also better value for the client over the long term.

Active ingredients	Radiesse ™ is composed of tiny synthetic calcium hydroxylapatite (CaHA) microspheres, suspended in a water-based gel carrier. The 25-40 micron diameter microspheres, once injected, provide a scaffold stimulating collagen production around the microspheres, and into which, the body's own tissue can grow, thereby maintaining the implant in situ and ensuring continued volumisation.
Indications	Full face volumisaiton, nasolabials, cheekbone enhancements, jawline(mandibular-mental) enhancement, marionette lines, nasal augmentation(bridge, columella and nasal tip)
Persistence:	Approximately 12+ months
Appearance	Gel
Storage	Room temperature (30°C)
Origin	Synthetic
Pre-test required	No
Manufacturer	RADIESSE Worldwide – European Office Everdenberg 11 4902 TT Oosterhout (NBr) The Netherlands Tel: +31.162.474.800

Sculptra®

Newfill/Sculptra®

This product is used for treating large defects such as hollows in the cheeks, reshaping the chin and jaw line, and increasing tissue volume of the face. Treatment outcome is unpredictable and most patients require at least four treatments which can be costly.

Active ingredients	Poly-L-lactic acid
Additional ingredients	CMC (carboxymethylcellulose), mannitol, water.
Mode of action (according to manufacturer)	The filling action is immediate simply due to the straightforward mechanical effect, related to the quantity of material injected and continues over the longer term due to the slow resorption of the polylactic acid over a period of several months, leading to the appearance of a fibrous dermal layer prolonging its effect
Indications	Wrinkles, marked furrows or creases
Persistence:	Approximately 15-18 months
Appearance	Powder
Storage	Room temperature (30°C)
How supplied	2 vials of lyophilised L-PLA, 4 needles, 21G (2), and 26G (2)
Origin	Synthetic
Pre-test required	No
Manufacturer	Aventis House Kings Hill West Malling Kent PH: 44-7736 799945

Permanent Procedure

Artecoll

Active ingredients	Polymethylmethacrylate (PMMA) microspheres suspended in a solution of partly denatured 3.5% collagen.
Additional ingredients	0.3% lidocaine
Mode of action	Following the injection of artecoll in the lower part of the dermis (i.e. subdermally) body within 1-3 months. All the micro spheres will be totally encapsulated by a fine fibrous capsule. This process will be completed within 2-4 months after injections.
Volume	1.0 ml and 0.5 ml
Indications	Artecoll is used as an injectable micro-implant of the wrinkles and other defects in the connective tissue. The main indicators are folds, perioral liners, depressed corners of the mouth, lip augmentation, horizontal frontal furrows and acne scars. Artecoll should not be used for the fine lines.
Pre-Test Required	Yes
Origin	Bovine Collagen and Polymethylmethacrylate
Manufacturer	Rofil Medical International B.V., Internat. Stadionstraat 1B, 4815 NC Breda, The Netherlands

Dermalive

Active ingredients	Acrylic Hydrogel 200mg = Hydroxylmethacrylat (HEMA) and Ethylmethacrylat (EMA) copolymerised. Crosslinked hyaluronic acid 14.4mg
Definition	Dermalive is a suspension of flexible, non-resorbable fragments of acrylic hydrogel in a sterile, non-pyrogenic and physiological solution of slightly crosslinked non-animal hyaluronic acid. The hyaluronic acid serves only as a carrier of the implant. The acrylic hydrogel fragments, 60 mm in diameter on average, are large enough not to migrate and not to be engulfed by phagocytes. Acrylic hydrogel belongs to the acrylate family. The name "Hydrogel" is because of the water content, 26% in Dermalive.
Additional ingredients	Phosphate buffer
Volume of syringe	0.6 ml
Appearance	White gel
Indications	Cutaneous depressions such as naso-labial fold, bitterness wrinkles, puckering of lips, soft tissue augmentation in cheeks and chin, correcting scars and rhinoplasty.
Storage	Stored at a temperature of between 2–8oC
How supplied	Dermalive is supplied in a box with one syringe 0.6 ml together with a sterile 271/2 G needle.
Origin	Non-animal hyaluronic acid + acrylic fragments
Pre-Test Required	No
Manufacturer	Dermatech, 28 rue de Caumartin, 75 009 Paris, France.

Botulinum Toxin (Botox® Injections)

The cosmetic form of botulinum toxin often referred to by its product name Botox® is a popular non-surgical injection that temporarily reduces or eliminates frown lines, forehead creases, crow's feet near the eyes and thick bands in the neck. The toxin blocks the nerve impulses, temporarily paralysing the muscles that cause wrinkles while giving the skin a smoother, more refreshed appearance. There are several different types of botulinum toxin, and the currently marketed therapeutic toxin is type A. Presently, there are only few manufacturers of Type A botulinum toxin. The three most used products are listed below.

Product	Manufacturer	Product	Approved for Cosmetic use
Botox®	Allergan, Inc. P.O. Box 19534 Irvine, CA 92623 USA Tel: (714) 246-4500 Fax: (714) 246-4971	Botox® Vistabe® is approved for cosmetic use for glabellar lines only. Botox is not approved for cosmetic use.	Vistabel® is approved for cosmetic use only for the glabellar lines.
Dysport®	Wigmore Medical 23 Wigmore Street, London T: 2074910190	Dysport ®is approved for the treatment of blepharospasm, hemi facial spasm, spasmodic torticollis and other non-cosmetic uses.	?
Xeomin®	Merz 260 Centennial Park Elstree Hill South Elstree Hertfordshire WD6 3SR T:02082363516	Xeomin® is the third type of botulinum toxin type A available in the UK market. The company claims that the complex proteins have been removed through a complex purification process making the product much safer than the existing products on the market.	?

Bio – Stimulation Treatments

Mesotherapy is the most popular bio-stimulation treatment today.

What is Mesotherapy?

Mesotherapy is the unique combination of art and science developed by Dr. Michel Pistor of Paris, France in 1952. It is a medical specialty using painless microinjections of vitamins, herbs, homeopathic remedies and pharmaceuticals in specific formulations. Mesotherapy can be applied to a multitude of different conditions, both medical and cosmetic.

What is involved?

A series of micro-injections with a unique formulation of vitamins are injected into the mesoderm of the skin.

Mesotherapy for facial rejuvenation allows the true restructuring of the skin tissue since the formulation has been fully designed to favour the different biological reactions of the architecture of the skin by supplements:

- The vitamins provide an anti-deficiency function.

- The amino acids allow better protein construction.

- The minerals guarantee the ionic balance of the medium.

- The coenzymes activate the biochemical reactions.

- The nucleic acids stimulate synthesis.

When does the client see results?

Most patients see results immediately after their first treatment.

Is Mesotherapy for facial rejuvenation permanent?

No, because we continue to age. If the client likes the results, they will most likely continue with a few sessions annually. This treatment is becoming increasingly popular in the United Kingdom.

Why does the client need more than one treatment?

Mesotherapy for facial rejuvenation is usually performed in an initial series of 2 - 4 treatments spaced 2 – 3 weeks apart. The effects of the treatment are cumulative. Your body will slowly develop collagen and elastin over time.

What Are The Risks?

There is a very small chance of bruising which can easily be covered.

What will the treatment do for the client?

The treatment is a bio revitalizing treatment. By injecting hyaluronic acid and other nutrients into the dermis, the client will notice a visibly improvement in the tone, hydration and texture of their skin.

How often does the client need to have the treatment to maintain the results?

At least every 3-4 months

Mesotherapy for Fat and Cellulite Reduction

Cellulite Treatment

Cellulite troubles the overwhelming majority of women in their lifetime. It has very little to do with obesity, for the thin, slender women may also be affected. Until the advent of mesotherapy, its treatment has been most difficult if not virtually impossible. Liposuction has failed to correct this condition.

The specific mesotherapy formula of nutrients for cellulite treatment will provide the following benefits:

- Improves circulation both venous and lymphatic.
- Removes connective tissue bands, which give the "cottage cheese" appearance to the thighs.
- Dissolves fat lobules trapped between these bands and thus creates a tight smooth skin surface.

■ Improves lymphatic drainage and circulation which helps to improve the appearance of the treated area.

Meostherapy for Fat Reduction

Mesotherapy for Fat Reduction works similarly to cellulite treatment except fewer products are used to treat the condition. There is no need to treat the thick collagen bands.

There are approximately six categories of treatments which involve different areas of medicine. Many medical aesthetic solutions are duplications of each other, and many treatments and products are new with no clinical data demonstrating safety and efficacy. Therefore, there is no need to provide unlimited treatments and products. Pick the best products in each category and become an expert with these treatments. By developing expertise with a small group of core procedures, you will become better at delivering predictable treatment outcomes. It is true that cosmetic clients will ask for certain products or treatments but if you and your staff explain to the client the reason the clinic does not provide the requested product or treatment, the client will accept your decision, especially if the product is unsafe or unproven.

The products and treatments listed in this book are evidence based with solid track records of success. Unlike traditional medicine, there is no need to experiment with new products. My advice is to evaluate any new product or treatment over a few years before you introduce new options to your clients, especially if the new product is a duplication of an existing product. Do not use your clients as test models on behalf of the new manufacturer.

The affinity diagram demonstrates that each category of treatments will treat different skin problems. In most cases, it will take one treatment from each category to achieve ultimate results. Clients do not understand that there isn't a perfect product so it is important that you use the affinity diagram to demonstrate how the integration of different treatment options will work together to achieve optimum results.

1.8 Procedure Pricing

These are approximate prices which can be used as a reference however, you may want to review with your supplier to confirm that there are no changes before you begin to create your financial forecast.

Procedures	Cost to Patient	Direct Cost	Time Required/ hours	Gross Margin
Consultation Fee	£0.00	£0.00	0.5	0.00%
Chemical Peel-AHA	£70.00	£3.00	0.5	95.71%
Series of 4 treatments	£230.00	£12.00	2	94.78%
Series of 6 treatments	£350.00	£18.00	3	94.86%
TCA-Easy Peel	£599.00	£88.13	2	85.29%
Dermal Fillers				
Hydrafill/Juvaderm-1syringe	£300.00	£80	0.5	73%
Hydrafill/Juvaderm-2 syringes	£500.00	£160.00	0.75	68%
Hydrafill/Juvaderm-Additional Syringes	£200.00	£80.00	0.2	60%
Restylane-1syringe	£350.00	£100.00	0.5	71.43%
Additional Syringes £200	£200.00	£100.00	0.5	50.00%
Perlane-1 syringe	£350.00	£105.00	0.5	70.00%
Botox®				
1 unit	£5.00	£1.40	0.25	72.00%
30	£150.00	£42.00	0.25	72.00%
40	£200.00	£56.00	0.25	72.00%
50	£250.00	£70.00	0.4	72.00%
60	£300.00	£84.00	0.5	72.00%
70	£350.00	£98.00	0.5	72.00%
80	£400.00	£112.00	0.5	72.00%
90	£450.00	£126.00	0.5	72.00%
100	£500.00	£140.00	0.5	72.00%
Mesotherapy				
Facial Rejuvenation				
1st treatment (individual/maintenance)	£120.00	£20.00	0.5	83.33%

Procedures	Cost to Patient	Direct Cost	Time Required/ hours	Gross Margin
2nd	£100.00	£20.00	0.5	80.00%
3rd	£80.00	£20.00	0.5	75.00%
4th	£70.00	£20.00	0.5	71.43%
Mesotherapy(body)				
Cellulite Treatment (1 area or individual)	£100.00	£20.00	0.5	80.00%
Cellulite Treatment (2 areas)	£180.00	£40.00	0.5	77.78%
Cellulite Treatment (3 areas)	£250.00	£50.00	0.5	80.00%
Fat Reduction (1 area or individual)	£100.00	£20.00	0.5	80.00%
Fat Reduction (2 areas or individual)	£180.00	£40.00	0.5	77.78%
Fat Reduction (3 areas)	£250.00	£40.00	0.5	84.00%
Radiesse™				
1st treatment (1 vial)	£400.00	£80.00	0.5	80%
1st treatment (2 vials)	£700.00	£160.00	0.75	78%
Additional Syringes	£250	£80..00	.25	68%

135

To Do List

- Identify growth procedures in both surgical and non surgical markets

- Establish realistic financial objectives for each business unit

- Establish the key suppliers of non-surgical aesthetic products

- Establish a concrete growth plan for each business unit

- Establish an efficient procedure strategy for entering the aesthetic market

- Establish a pricing policy for the major non-invasive procedures

- Establish core and secondary responsibilities for your staff

- Identify your training and development consultant

Chapter 2

Client Relationship Management

Your specialty will determine the quality of your cosmetic base. In most practices, one in five patients is a possible candidate for a number of aesthetic procedures. If you are new to aesthetic medicine the best place to start recruiting clients is in your practice. Your present patients know and trust you so a relationship is already established. This is the best place to start. If the treatment is less than perfect, your present patient will be more forgiving and will most likely give you a second chance instead of going elsewhere. But to develop this market you need to focus more on client relationship.

In traditional medicine, medical practices do not have to be concerned about patient acquisition and patient relationship. The demand for your service is more than you can supply. Consequently, patients wait for days to get an appointment, have to take time off work to keep their appointment, tolerate long waiting times, sit in a grungy waiting room, and tolerate impolite office staff. However, when a patient becomes a cosmetic client, they are aware that the cosmetic service you provide is available elsewhere, and although they trust and like you, they will go elsewhere if you do not make the necessary adjustments to improve client relationships. You need to find out your patients' expectations and value systems.

When I say expectations and value systems, I am not just referring to the treatment. Other services, such as follow-up calls, flexible appointments, after-hour services, weekend services and free parking are major contributors to the whole treatment experience and can determine if a client will remain loyal to your practice. The keystone to your practice growth is your clients' needs and wants. Find out what your clients expect from you.

Most client-centric companies, large or small, are employing new client relationship management software technologies to enhance the overall profitability of their business and ensure long-term advantage over their competitor. These new CRM (client relationship management) software solutions enable business-to-consumer companies to manage, track, resolve and report on client feedback from all channels, which ultimately allow companies to excel in every different aspect of their client relationship management approach.

I am not recommending that new clinicians invest in expensive CRM software solutions to stay ahead of the competition. I want to impress on you the complexity of this subject and provide alternative solutions for your business. I have listed the more important areas of client relationship management that should be taken into consideration. For those clinicians who do not understand the value of customer relationship, I will demonstrate the importance of this subject by referring to the charts below.

Dermal Filler Projection- Year 1

	Jan	Feb	Mar	Apr	May	Jun	Jul	Aug	Sept	Oct	Nov	Dec
New Patients	5	5	5	5	5	5	5	5	5	5	5	5
Revenue from new patients (£275/treatment)												
	1375	1375	1375	1375	1375	1375	1375	1375	1375	1375	1375	1375
Revenue from returning patients (£)												
							1375	1375	1375	1375	1375	1375
Monthly total revenue for year 1 (£)												
	1375	1375	1375	1375	1375	1375	2750	2750	2750	2750	2750	2750
Total dermal filler revenue in Year 1 = £24,750												

Dermal Filler Projection- Year 2

	Jan	Feb	Mar	Apr	May	Jun	Jul	Aug	Sept	Oct	Nov	Dec
New Patients	5	5	5	5	5	5	5	5	5	5	5	5
Previous year Patients												
Jan-Jun	5	5	5	5	5	5	5	5	5	5	5	5
Jul-Aug	5	5	5	5	5	5	5	5	5	5	5	5
Present Year Patients												
Jan-Jun							5	5	5	5	5	5
Total	15	15	15	15	15	15	20	20	20	20	20	20
Total Year 2 Revenue = 210 treatments at £275/treatment = £57,750												

In the first half of year one, the practice treated only new clients which can be coded as NDF (new dermal filler). In the second half of the year, at least 50% of the clients in months July to December should be EDF clients (existing dermal filler clients)

In the first half of year two, 2/3 of clients treated should be EDF (existing dermal filler clients). In the latter half of the year, at least 75 % of dermal filler clients should be repeating clients.

It is important that this type of ratio exists to protect the long term success of the business. Analysis of how you earn your income is necessary to minimize future financial risks.

Many clinicians have done well so far by treating only new patients without any consideration to customer relationship management or customer retention because of past excess demand for medical aesthetic services. Today, competition is fierce and the cost to attract new customers is rising exponentially. Case study 1 on page 53 demonstrates the cost of client generation. The costs of web site development, web optimization, yellow-page advertisement, magazine advertisement etc.... are rising by the hour. Therefore, it is far less expensive to improve your customer service strategy to keep the clients you presently have.

Large and medium size clinics should invest in innovative contact management software to measure client retention. By month six, the information provided by the reporting component of the software will inform you of customer loyalty, allowing you to fix problems early. Below is a list of other areas that the software will help you to continually improve your practice performance. The following subjects are very important in customer relations. No cost is too little to ensure that you are aware of the business performance. It is more expensive to find new customers than it is to keep an existing customer. It is better to know your inefficiencies sooner than later.

Contact management software: Client information, which includes demographics and buying habits, is vital for developing the practice's financial forecast and marketing objectives. Without this information, you cannot plan effectively. In chapter1, section 1.6, I discussed the importance of planning and financial forecasting. In the first year of business, you will not have any quantitative data available so you will develop the forecast with qualitative information only. However, in year two, it is expected that the practice will have some quantitative data relating to the clinic's previous year's performance. Revenue should be segmented by functional departments to identify areas of weakness.

The best software we have found so far which can be configured to measure almost every aspect of a clinic's performance is ACT. The software does require modification, but it is far superior to any medical software that I have seen including the E-Clinic software. Dentistry software appears to be more sophisticated and many have the capability to establish codes for customers. This is a great tracking device to evaluate customer retention.

Client retention: I cannot say this enough; you need to establish a system to track client retention. Do not assume that everyone you treat will return. You need quantitative data on how well your clients like you and the service you provide. To maintain contact with your clients, you need to follow up with clients, send reminders, communicate new procedures through e-mail, and track your client's consumption of your services. You cannot accomplish this task without automation. Our business courses will teach practice managers and practice owners these skills.

Front office management

Call management: how are calls managed? Is the receptionist the only person responsible for incoming calls? The telephone should be answered by the third ring. Ask your receptionist if this is the case. If the practice is not dedicated to aesthetic medicine, I doubt all calls are answered by the third ring. In this case, you may want to have all aesthetic calls answered by a cosmetic receptionist or a call centre dedicated to managing cosmetic inquiries. You can set up a web base diary, which the call centre can use to book your appointments. Your inside staff can also access the diary in the event that they should need to book cosmetic consultations as well.

Call capture: how many incoming calls are actually answered? Approximately, 50% of all cosmetic calls go unanswered because the receptionist is too busy and physicians and their staff still assume that aesthetic clients will call back. This is not the case, and unless you know your call capture rate, you have no idea how much business you are losing on a daily basis. It is surprising how much money physicians spend on promotion yet overlook this area of their operation. Outsource your inbound cosmetic calls to a source that can provide you with solid quantitative data on how well the phone is being managed.

Call logging: do you have any system set up to track all incoming calls? Your monthly phone bill can provide you with this information but this is not enough. When someone calls your phone line, they are interested in buying and all that is required is a trained receptionist to answer and convert the call to a booked consultation. It is impossible for the receptionist to sell services if the first point of contact is inefficient. All your marketing efforts are lost here. This is a common mistake with many practices.

Client Satisfaction

Client feedback: information needed to develop your marketing strategy. It only makes sense that you try to find out how your clients feel about your service. There are only few clinicians able to give me quantitative information on customer satisfaction. It is assumed that clients are satisfied. Follow up calls after every treatment is important even for repeat clients. On a quarterly basis, it is not a bad idea to hold a round table discussion with your most valuable clients and your staff. Find out what areas of the practice they feel can be improved. This is the perfect opportunity to evaluate if your concept of your clinic is consistent with how the customer sees you. It is a good exercise for your staff as well. I know that it is unusual to have clients evaluate you but your aesthetic business is also a commercial business, and therefore, it is mandatory that you know how your customers feel about you.

Complaint handling: policies should be outlined in your operations manual and complaints should be documented and reviewed monthly. Most of us do not like to handle complaints, but it is a necessary evil. Follow-up calls, effective pre and post consultation protocols, setting realistic expectations, taking your time with the client, listening to the client, and before and after photographs will definitely help in reducing customer complaint.

I embrace complaints because the customer is making an attempt to communicate with me. Most customers do not complain - they find it easier to move on and tell others about the poor service they received. Address all complaints and try your best to solve the problem. The clinician will know if the client is a complainer or is making a legitimate complaint. If the clinician is not the practice owner, the clinician may sometimes view complaints as a criticism of their work so it is best that the complaint is handled by the business owner. I have dealt with many complaints where the client had legitimate reasons for complaining because the clinician's attitude and work ethics were poor.

Client loyalty: information on client loyalty should be tracked and should be taken into consideration as part of your marketing strategy. Client loyalty can be described in a number of ways: a long time client who utilizes just one service, long time client who uses multiple services, long time - infrequent client, long time client who sends referrals, new client (less than one year) with high life time value potential, new client who sends referrals etc...You need to evaluate the types of customers you presently have. To increase revenue, you do not necessarily have to attract new clients, you can establish internal marketing strategies to motivate lower tier clients (minimal loyalty) into becoming more loyal clients by motivating them to send referrals and use more services provided by the practice.

Introducing credit facility is the most effective means of motivating lower tier clients to use more services. I have provided you with a lot of information on your potential clients' needs and wants but this should not stop you from finding out more about your market segment's needs and wants. The philosophy in my company is to over-deliver. Therefore, I have a 95% assurance that all my customers are satisfied. I also make all of my clients complete an evaluation form at the end of a course or project, and I am always surprised to see the comments. Sometimes we do miss things, and we quickly rectify. I never want myself and my staff to think that we are perfect and untouchable. We are continually striving for excellence. Our business has increased from prior year by 300% due to customer loyalty and referrals. We do not advertise. My husband is a genius with web marketing and my staff members are without a doubt dedicated to customer service. Our company prides itself on Relationship Marketing and our success is directly related to this philosophy of over-delivering to our customers.

Client support: do you have guidelines established on client support and are these guidelines established in your operation manual? I recently provided consulting services for a surgeon. I noticed that many of his surgical clients were not from the local area and their partners sometimes needed to stay over night in the area where surgery was scheduled. The cost for an overnight stay in the hospital is £400/night. Also, a few clients were unable to coordinate transportation back to their homes-post surgery.

This is such a simple problem. However, no one in the practice felt it was his or her responsibility to coordinate this client support system. In fact, the office manager felt that by providing these services for clients, the practice was opening up a can of worms. I felt differently. In fact, I organized for a local taxi company to quote a standard price for transporting cosmetic clients back to their homes (only those who needed it), and I negotiated a corporate daily rate of £85 with a hotel close to the hospital. Clients wanting to stay overnight can use the practice's corporate reference number to receive the special room rate. Within one month, the practice booked four surgical patients who would not have booked if this service were not available.

The reason the office manager did not want to take on this responsibility is that it added additional responsibilities to her already large workload. A lot of times, staff members feel undervalued and underpaid, and therefore, they are not prepared to go out of their way to take on more work on behalf of the practice. Customer Service Training, an effective team bonus, and individual bonus plan (discussed in chapter 3) will certainly help to motivate staff members to support cosmetic clients.

Respond system: how effective is your practice in responding to client inquiries and do you have guidelines established to monitor your response efficiency?

Client intelligence: information on your market segments should be tracked and linked to your marketing strategy.

Client Surveys

An effective client survey cannot capture all the information provided by CRM software technology but until you are ready to invest in CRM software, I would recommend you conduct an effective survey with your existing client base and with new clients. These will give you a lot of information to develop your future client service and sales strategies.

Topics to be covered in the survey
- Patient demographics
- Patient psychographics
- Waiting times
- After hours service
- Time spent with the doctor
- Quality of your nursing staff
- Additional services required
- Practice environment
- Parking facilities
- Communication with physician and practice staff
- Billing issues
- Appointment management
- Front desk management
- Client support

Cover letter for client survey questionnaire

Here is an example of the kind of covering message that should accompany your Client Management Survey.

Dear Patient

The Your-Name Centre of Excellence is dedicated to providing its clients with the highest quality health care in a private, compassionate, and cost-effective manner.

We need your help to evaluate our effectiveness and to initiate changes in areas that require improvement.

Please take a few minutes to complete the survey. Your answers and suggestions will help us to continually improve the service we provide to you.

I thank you in advance for your support.

Use the template as a model and tailor it to your specific situation.

"This may seem simple, but you need to give customers what they want, not what you think they want. And, if you do this, people will keep coming back".
John Ilhan

Client Management Survey

About yourself	
Name:	Date of Birth
Sex	Occupation
Address:	
e-mail address:	This is an important piece of information that needs to be recorded in the patient file. Communication with clients is much easier and effective via e-mail.
Marital Status:	Gender: Male ☐ Female ☐

Our Specialty and Services
1) Are you familiar with the range of services we offer? Yes ☐ No ☐
2) What procedures are of interest to you? Liposuction ☐   Face Lifts ☐   Lower Face Lifts ☐ AHA Peels ☐   Chemical Peels ☐   Laser Resurfacing ☐ Laser Hair Removal ☐   Botox® ☐   Dermal Fillers ☐ Thermage ☐   Skin Care ☐   Isolagen ☐
3) Have you had any of these procedures elsewhere? Yes ☐ No ☐
If answer is yes, please provide details:
4) Do you have a personal aesthetician? Yes ☐ No ☐
Would it be more convenient if aesthetic services were provided here? Yes ☐ No ☐
Please list services:

5) Would you like to receive information on the treatment listed above? Yes ☐ No ☐
Please list procedures:

Office Environment

6) Do you find our waiting room comfortable? Yes ☐ No ☐
If no, expand:

7) Do you feel relaxed in our waiting room? Yes ☐ No ☐
If no, expand:

8) Are our parking facilities adequate?
If no, expand:

Office Personnel

9a) Do you find our front office personnel (secretary, receptionist):
Friendly: Yes ☐ No ☐   Courteous: Yes ☐ No ☐

9b) Knowledgeable on services: Excellent ☐ Good ☐ Poor ☐

10a) Do you find our business personnel (office manager)
Friendly: Yes ☐ No ☐   Courteous: Yes ☐ No ☐

10b) Knowledgeable on services: Excellent ☐ Good ☐ Poor ☐

11) Are your phone calls handled in a prompt courteous manner?
Yes ☐ No ☐

Nurse Clinician

Do you find our nurse clinician:

12a) Friendly: Yes ☐ No ☐

12b) Courteous: Yes ☐ No ☐

13) Did the nurse give you enough information about the procedure you are interested in?
Yes ☐ No ☐

Doctor

Do you find the doctor:

14a) Friendly: Yes ☐ No ☐

14b) Courteous: Yes ☐ No ☐

15) Did the doctor give you enough information about the procedure you are interested in?
Yes ☐ No ☐

16) Did the doctor spend enough time with you?
Yes ☐ No ☐

Scheduling and Waiting Time

17) Is the waiting time too long?
Yes ☐ No ☐

18) Do you have problems getting an appointment as soon as you would like?
Yes ☐ No ☐

19) Do you have difficulties in finding appointments that meet your needs?
Yes ☐ No ☐

How would you make improvements in this area?

Fees Structure

Do you feel that our fees are:
20a) High ☐ 20b) Average ☐ 20c)Low ☐

21) Are you familiar with our credit and billing policies?
Yes ☐ No ☐

Service

22) Are you satisfied with the range of services provided by this practice?
Yes ☐ No ☐

23) Are there specific services that you would like to see us provide? Yes ☐ No ☐
Please list:

24a) How were you referred to this practice?
Yellow Pages ☐ Magazine Article ☐ Newspaper ☐
Referral ☐ Live in the area ☐ Other ☐

24b) Are you familiar with our Patient Referral Program?
Yes ☐ No ☐

24c) Would you like to receive information on our Patient Referral Program?
Yes ☐ No ☐

Please use this space for any additional comments you may have:

Signature:

Data analysis method

- Record the total number of Yes and No responses by question

- Record the percentages of the Yes, No, Excellent, Good, Fair

Responses for each question

- Calculate the percentage - divide the number of Yes, No, Excellent, Good, Fair responses by the total number and multiply by 100.

- Record the Yes, No, Excellent, Good, Fair percentages for each question (refer to Tabulation Sheet)

- Assign a marketing priority number to each question.

Response Percentage	Priority
0 –25	4
26 –51	3
51 –75	2
76 –100	1

Tabulation Sheet

Questions	Yes	No	% Yes	% No
1	100	400	20%	80%
2				
Liposuction	50	450	10%	90%
Face Lifts	30	470	6%	94%
Lower Face Lifts	30	470	6%	94%
AHA Peels	130	370	26%	74%
Chemical Peels	35	365	7%	93%
Laser Resurfacing	25	425	5%	95%
Laser Hair Removal	50	450	10%	90%
Botox®	300	200	60%	40%
Dermal Fillers	135	365	27%	73%
Thermage	0	500	0	100%
Skin Care	200	300	40%	60%
Isolagen	350	150	70%	30%
3	300	200	60%	40%
4	400	100	80%	20%
5	400	100	80%	20%
6	200	300	40%	60%
7	200	300	40%	60%
8	250	250	50%	50%
9a	150	350	30%	70%
9b	200	300	40%	60%
10a	150	350	30%	70%
10b	200	300	40%	60%
11	150	350	30%	70%
12a	100	400	20%	80%
12b	200	300	40%	60%
13	250	250	50%	50%
14a	300	200	60%	40%
14b	400	100	80%	20%
15	300	200	60%	40%
16	200	300	40%	60%
17	400	100	80%	20%
18	450	50	90%	10%
19	300	200	605	40%
20				
A-High	300		60%	
B-Average	100		20%	
C- Low	100		20%	
21	250	250	50%	50%
22	275	225	55%	45%
23	Leave			
24a	Leave			
24b	100	400	20%	80%
24c	100	400	20%	80%

Analysis Sheet

Questions	Description	Yes	No	Priority
1	Familiar with services	20%	80%	1
2 Liposuction Face Lifts Lower Face Lifts AHA Peels Chemical Peels Laser Resurfacing Laser Hair Removal Botox® Dermal Fillers Thermage Skin Care Isolagen	Information request	10% 6% 6% 26% 7% 5% 10% 60% 27% 0 40% 70%	90% 94% 94% 74% 93% 95% 90% 40% 73% 100% 60% 30%	4 4 4 3 4 4 4 3 3 4 3 2
3	Have you had procedure elsewhere	60%	40%	-
4	Do you have aesthetician	80%	20%	1
5	Would you like information	80%	20%	1
6	Waiting Room	40%	60%	2
7	Relaxed in waiting room	40%	60%	2
8	Parking	50%	50%	3
9a 9b	Front Staff	30% 40%	70% 60%	2 2
10a 10b	Office manager	30% 40%	70% 60%	2 2
11	Phone Calls	30%	70%	2
12a 12b	Nurse's friendliness	20% 40%	80% 60%	1 2
13	Info provided by nurse	50%	50%	3
14a 14b	Doctor's attitude	60% 80%	40% 20%	3 4
15	Info provided by Doctor	60%	40%	3
16	Time spent by doctor	40%	60%	2
17	Waiting Time	80%	20%	1
18	Flexible appointments	90%	10%	1
19	Appt. that meet needs	60%	40%	2
20 A-High B-Average C- Low		60% 20% 20%		2
21	Billing Policies	50%	50%	3
22	Range of Services	55%	45%	2
23	Leave			
24a 24b 24c	Referral Program	20%	80%	1

153

Marketing issues identified

Weaknesses

■ Patients not familiar with the range of services - develop plan to educate patients.

■ Focus more efforts on non-invasive procedures

■ Provide patients with more information on each service offered at the clinic.

■ Develop a quarterly newsletter

■ Improve the appearance of the waiting room.

■ Retrain front staff.

■ Retrain the office manager

■ Retrain nurses on client relationship.

■ Improve scheduling efficiency to minimise waiting time.

■ Develop a Patient Referral Program. (discussed in chapter five)

Strengths

■ Parking is convenient.

■ Doctor-patient communication is above average.

■ Billing-patient communication is above average.

This information will be the meat of your marketing plan. Without knowing what your clients like and do not like about you, it is difficult to develop a client centric marketing strategy. Review the survey thoroughly, and you and your team need to spend some time to develop creative ways to improve the service to your clients without incurring additional cost.

Chapter one-subject covered

- Growth procedure for all market segments
- How to develop marketing and financial budgets
- Key suppliers of non-surgical aesthetic products
- Growth plan for each business unit
- Established pricing policy for the core non-surgical procedures
- Established core and secondary responsibilities for your staff
- Identified outside resources to assist you in procedure training and business development

Chapter two-subject covered

- Client Retention
- Call Logging
- Client follow-up
- Call response system
- Call capture rate
- Client feedback
- Client complaint
- Client loyalty
- Client support
- Customer Survey

Chapter 3

Staff Development

Hire the right staff

It is safe to say that the vision of every aesthetic clinician is one where clients prefer your service to the unlimited possibilities that exist out there. However, implementing this vision comes with just one catch: you cannot do it alone. You will need the help of others. The bottom line is you have to surround yourself with talented people, or else you are not going to accomplish what you want. The question is - how do you recognise talented people?

The best place to begin is to hire the right people for the job. The greatest football trainer could not be successful if his goalkeeper could not stop the ball, his backs could not defend, and his forwards could not attack. When you have selected your key individuals, you must provide the necessary training to home in on their natural abilities. This comes with practice and leadership. To be a successful team everyone must be a team player. You are the team leader, and you must invest time in selecting the right people to be a part of this team. They must understand the overall strategy of the practice and be prepared to be involved in achieving these objectives in their everyday performance.

I would like to share with you a summarized version of a presentation made by Dr. Peter Ilori on people development. Mr. Ilori is a businessman, Orthodontist and a great leader of people. (Beauty Society, Octagon Orthodontics, Beauty in Colour and The Beauty Society magazine). As one of his consultants it was very easy to integrate new strategies within his practice since his people were motivated and participated in the execution of planned activities. He is one of the few physicians that understands leadership and puts it into practice.

Presentation Summary-Peter Ilori

Profitability is the resultant of getting things done

Profitability = Fees received – Expenses

Your Staff is responsible for:

- Receiving your fees
- Controlling your expenses
- Influencing time taken to execute daily activities

Why are overseas companies 20-40% more productive than their UK Counterparts?

Because they are more:

- Pro-active in investing in and developing their people.

- Your people represent one of your major sources of sustainable competitive advantage.

- Clear links exist between the way your people are managed and your business performance.

- Higher levels of performance, profitability & customer satisfaction can be achieved by enhancing your people & engaging their enthusiasm.

Profitability = Fees received – Expenses

Time Taken

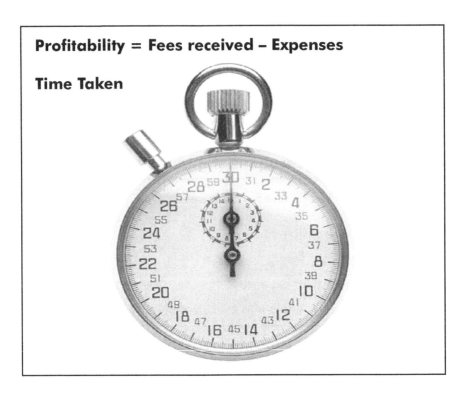

Time Taken = efficiency

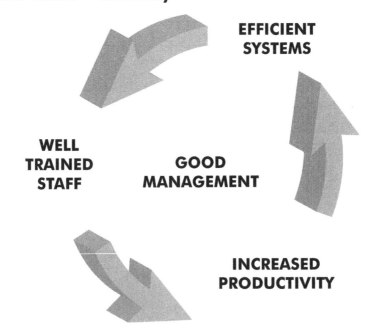

EFFICIENT SYSTEMS

WELL TRAINED STAFF

GOOD MANAGEMENT

INCREASED PRODUCTIVITY

Efficiency = staff motivation

Staff motivation = Job satisfaction

Staff turn-over is a problem when the economy and jobs market are strong

Retention has **nothing to do with salary**. It's to do with working in an organisation **you feel part of**, rather than the old-fashioned factory environment.

(Colin Osborne of consultants CMG, Quoted in Massey in 1995)

Motivation: what does staff want?

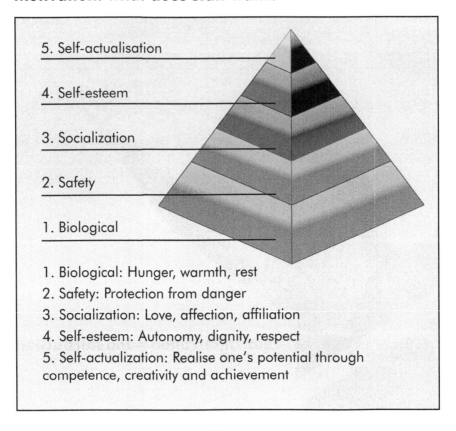

5. Self-actualisation

4. Self-esteem

3. Socialization

2. Safety

1. Biological

1. Biological: Hunger, warmth, rest
2. Safety: Protection from danger
3. Socialization: Love, affection, affiliation
4. Self-esteem: Autonomy, dignity, respect
5. Self-actualization: Realise one's potential through competence, creativity and achievement

How do you motivate staff?

- Hold regular meetings where employees can express their views
- Introduce training programmes
- Find out what motivates your staff as individuals
- Create a blame free environment so staff can learn from their mistakes
- Make employees feel involved in the company's objectives.

Can you control time?

- Invest in staff training
- Examine your business processes critically
- Buy technology that saves time
- Decrease your overall treatment time

Dr. Ilori presentation implies that practice profitability is linked to the staff. A practice does not have to only focus on increasing revenue to increase profit. A practice can improve the efficiency of its staff which will impact the present profitability of the business. To do so the practice owner needs to focus on proper selection of staff, training, and motivating staff members to manage time efficiently. I am a strong believer in staff development and in this section of the book, I will provide you with tips on how to select, train, and motivate staff members to perform at their highest level.

In this section of the book, we will discuss the following:

- Effective job placement advertisements.
- Interviewing questions.
- Subjects to be covered in the Employee Operational Manual.
- Remuneration structure.
- Developing an Employee Training Manual.

3.1 Job Placement Advertisements

To attract the right people, you need to know in advance what you are looking for. You should have determined the following before you advertise the position:

■   The skill sets that are required by the individual.

■   The type of personality and appearance that you would like the individual to possess.

■   The salary range you are prepared to pay the right individual.

Below are examples of job placement advertisements for the three key positions in your practice.

Nurse

Professional nurse required for modern, dynamic, and successful medical cosmetic practice. This individual must have at least [x] years of medical aesthetic training and be able to work in a fast pace environment. The appropriate candidate should have superior interpersonal skills, and communication skills. Since this is an aesthetic position, sales and cosmetic experience is an asset.

The appropriate candidate should be prepared to be remunerated with a base salary (negotiable) and commission.

Please submit your CV with a covering letter stating why you are the appropriate candidate for this position to_____

_____

_____

_____

Receptionists/Sales Consultant

Professional Receptionist/Sales Consultant required for busy and successful medical cosmetic practice. This individual must have at least [x] years of experience working in a sales environment.

The right candidate should be mature, have excellent interpersonal skills, and be able to work in a fast paced environment. Sales and cosmetic experience is an asset.

The appropriate candidate should be prepared to be remunerated on a base salary and bonus system.

Please submit your CV with a covering letter stating why you are the appropriate candidate for this position to_____

_____

_____

_____

Practice Manager

She/he will be responsible for the overall operation of the practice. This involves:

■ Hiring and training office staff.

■ Overseeing the scheduling of appointments.

■ Overseeing billing requirements.

■ Motivating the team to keep track with sales objectives.

■ Reviewing sales performance on a daily basis.

■ Developing financial and marketing forecast

■ Managing expenses.

■ Project management skills (should be able to manage the launch of new procedures into the practice)

■ Good sales abilities (should be able to coach staff on vertical marketing and cross selling)

■ Leadership skills.

■ Analytical skills are mandatory in this job. You are looking for a business graduate, preferably with cosmetic experience.

■ Sales experience is a definite asset.

Professional Practice Manager required for busy and successful medical cosmetic practice. This individual must have at least [x] years of management experience.

The right candidate should possess strong leadership skills, supervisory skills, have superior interpersonal and communication skills, and be able to work in a fast-paced environment. Sales and cosmetic experience is an asset.

The appropriate candidate should be prepared to be remunerated with a base salary and a bonus system based on performance.

Please submit your CV with a covering letter stating why you are the appropriate candidate for this position to_____

_____

_____

_____

"If your thinking is sloppy, your business will be sloppy. If you are disorganized, your business will be disorganized. If you are greedy, your employees will be greedy, giving you less and less of themselves and always asking for more".
Michael Gerber

3.2 Interviewing Skills

Perfect candidates do not exist. Every candidate has strengths and liabilities. The ideal candidate is a highly subjective matter and will be different from one interviewer to another. The key here is to focus on the job requirements and not how well you got along with the candidate. Communication skills are highly important and should not be overlooked but this is not the only quality that you should be looking for. Before you meet with a candidate, determine the skill set that is required for the position. In the interview, observe the following:

Communication skills: How well does the candidate develop rapport with you? Do they build rapport by discussing the business, demonstrating common interests, asking questions about what you offer in the practice: e.g. is the practice dedicated to cosmetic medicine? Observe if the candidate is too friendly and talkative.

Demonstration of skills: A good candidate, aside from answering the questions you ask, should also be probing to find out what is important to be successful in the position. The candidate should be trying to demonstrate that their skills, experience and accomplishments are a perfect fit for the job requirements. If you do not know at present what is important for someone to be successful in the position, make sure that you do before you begin the interview.

Transferable skills: If the candidate does not have a specific skill set in an area, observe how well the individual can highlight other skills that will make up for this. For example, if I am asked the question "Do you have presentation skills?" and I do not, I will respond to the interviewer by asking, "How important is this skill to the position?" I would then say that I am proficient in putting together presentations, and I am willing to learn presentation skills in my own time. I would reiterate that I am not afraid to make presentations and I feel confident that, with practice, I can overcome this liability.

Salary expectations: Salary discussions are different from salary negotiations. Salary discussions typically centre on what the candidate made in previous positions or what the candidate is seeking to make in this position. If the candidate's prior salary or present expectations are in line with your salary offering, you have a better chance of keeping the appropriate individual happy and satisfied for a long period of time. If the salary expectation is more than you are prepared to pay, then you and the candidate need to negotiate compensation that is good for both of you. Remember, your team will contribute to the growth of the aesthetic component of your business, so be prepared to pay for talented individuals who offer a lifeline to the growth of your business.

Interview a number of people and do not be satisfied with the first individual that you mesh with. If you have an existing office manager, this individual can conduct the interview and shortlist the candidates. The ultimate decision will be yours. I have provided a template which you can use to interview candidates. For the nursing candidates, you will want to include the specific skills needed for the position. Include these in the template provided. Your office manager can carry out the interview and yourself and your office manager can interview the shortlist of candidates.

If you do not have an office manager or someone in the office that can conduct the interview, you will probably have to interview the candidates yourself. Possibly, make the appointment at the weekend and invest a day in interviewing candidates. Keep to the recommended questions as your guideline. Rehearse a bit so that the interview does not appear to be an interrogation. Remember the quality of your staff is the most important element in the overall success of the practice, so be very careful in making your selection. I am confident that the recommendations will improve the probability of you making the right choice.

Nurses

A highly skilled OR nurse who is trained to work in a stressful and emotional environment might not be appropriate for this industry. She might have all the right qualifications of an excellent nurse, someone you want at your side in the operating room, but if she has difficulty grasping the mission of the practice, understanding cosmetic clients' needs, and is not able to function in a cosmetic environment, it is best to pick a less skilled individual who can work in a cosmetic environment. I have noticed that skilled nurses with little appreciation for aesthetics are usually ineffective marketers. They might have the technical skills but lack the communication and commercial awareness that is needed to succeed in the aesthetic market.

Interview Questions for the Cosmetic Nurse

Employment Evaluation

Name...

Position: Cosmetic Nurse

Overall presentation: Good ☐ OK ☐ Poor ☐

Hair: Groomed ☐ Ungroomed ☐

Make-up: None ☐ Stylish ☐ Poor ☐

Tell me a little about yourself and your experience.

Answer should be a short summary of experience and some personal information. A good candidate should have researched the position and, if keen, should have asked themselves the question - "what does this job require?" Ideally, the person should match their skills with what you want. In addition, they should highlight other skills as a plus. This individual will have to demonstrate these skills when speaking to cosmetic clients.

Excellent ☐ Good ☐ Unprepared ☐ Ramble ☐

If the nurse has no cosmetic experience, ask what makes the candidate feel that they are appropriate for the position. Prior nursing experience is not enough to be effective in this position. Look to see if the candidate has any understanding of the position. Will she be confident in providing treatments to clients and can she sell multiple services to clients? This individual should not be afraid of making recommendations to clients.

Give me any example of a critical situation you have experienced and how you handled the situation.

Excellent patient care ☐ Problem solver ☐ OK ☐

The patients here are not sick but can be more difficult than hospital patients. For example, what if a patient called to complain about a procedure that you provided? How would you handle this situation?

Excellent ☐ Good ☐ OK ☐ Poor ☐

What do you know about cosmetic medicine?

You want to determine if this candidate is just looking for a job or is genuinely interested in this industry. The answer should show that they know something about what is required of them. Key descriptions: non-elective medicine, private patients, sales ability required, exciting environment, exceptional patient care required, patients are consumers and not patients.

Excellent ☐ Good ☐ OK ☐ Not a clue ☐

What do you know about the practice?

Hopefully some candidates looked up the practice on the web or in the phone book - looking for an answer that provides information on the range of procedures offered in the practice and the doctor's credentials.

Excellent ☐ Good ☐ OK ☐ Not a clue ☐

Staff in this practice has to work as a team and everyone's position is equally important. We also work on a salary and bonus system therefore you are required to promote the services of the practice. Are you comfortable with this?

Look for body language as an indication of their response to this question. You are looking for excitement at the opportunity of being paid for effort.

Excellent ☐ Good ☐ Negative ☐

Would you be able to make a presentation to a group of individuals on cosmetic medicine?

Answer should be "yes" or "yes, if I have the training and help with putting together the contents of the presentation".

Yes ☐ With training ☐ No ☐ Maybe ☐

In addition to your present nursing skills, we want you to be trained on other cosmetic procedures and to have you perform these procedures without doctor supervision. Are you willing to do so?

Yes ☐ No ☐ Maybe ☐

How do you feel about people wanting cosmetic procedures?

It's the individual's choice ☐ I have never thought of it really ☐

Would you consider having any kind of cosmetic treatment?

Yes ☐ No ☐ Possibly ☐ If I had the money ☐

Why should I hire you over another candidate?

A good candidate should have picked up on what you want and be able to relate your demands with her/his skills. The answer should be something like this: "Based on what you have said, you are looking for someone with these skills:..

I have all of these skills and more. In addition I can contribute in these areas:..

Cosmetic receptionists

Many physicians underestimate the skill and maturity of a good receptionist. The receptionist's job is one of the most important in a cosmetic practice since incoming calls are the lifeline to your practice. A well-trained receptionist will book more appointments, and educate potential patients about your credentials, your practice, and the benefits of choosing you over your competition. This is a very difficult job and only individuals with excellent people skills should be hired.

Interview Questions for the Cosmetic Receptionists

Employment Evaluation

Name..

Position: Receptionist

Overall presentation: Good ☐ OK ☐ Poor ☐

Hair: Groomed ☐ Ungroomed ☐

Make-up: None ☐ Stylish ☐ Poor ☐

Tell me a little about yourself and your experience.

Answer should be a short summary of experience and some personal information. What you are looking for is how succinctly the individual is able to present this information. In this industry, this person will have to present ideas and sales messages very efficiently.

Excellent ☐ Good ☐ Unprepared ☐ Ramble ☐

In your present job, give me an example of how do you deal with irate customers?

Excellent ☐ Good ☐ OK ☐ Poor ☐

Give me an example of a bad phone situation and how you were able to deal with it.

This is probably the most important question because the appropriate example will give you incredible insight on how this individual will handle crisis situations.

What motivates you the most in your present job?

You want to hear something like dealing with people, solving problems, educating the customers on our services.

Excellent ☐ Good ☐ OK ☐ Poor ☐

What do you know about cosmetic medicine?

You want to determine if this candidate is just looking for a job or genuinely interested in this industry. The answer should show that they know something about what is required of them. Key descriptions: non-elective medicine, paying patients, sales ability required, exciting environment, exceptional patient care required, and consumers not patients.

Excellent ☐ Good ☐ OK ☐ Not a clue ☐

What do you know about the practice?

Hopefully some candidates looked up the practice on the web or in the phone book - looking for an answer that provides information on the range of procedures offered in the practice and the doctor's credentials.

Excellent ☐ Good ☐ OK ☐ Not a clue ☐

Staff in this practice has to work as a team and everyone's position is equally important. We also work on a salary and bonus system therefore you are required to promote the services of the practice. Are you comfortable with this?

Look for body language as an indication of their response to this question. You are looking for excitement at the opportunity of being paid for effort.

Excellent ☐ Good ☐ Negative ☐

How do you feel about people wanting cosmetic procedures?

It's the individual's choice ☐ I've never thought about it ☐

Would you have anything done to yourself?

Yes ☐ No ☐ Possibly ☐ If I had the money ☐

Why should I hire you over another candidate?

A good candidate should have picked up on what you want and be able to relate your demands with her/his skills. The answer should be something like this: Based on what you have said, you are looking for someone with these skills:...

I have all of these skills and more. In addition I can contribute in these areas:...

Practice Manager

Employment Evaluation

Name...

Overall presentation: Good ☐ OK ☐ Poor ☐

Hair: Groomed ☐ Ungroomed ☐

Make-up: None ☐ Stylish ☐ Poor ☐

If the individual is not presentable, do not continue with the interview. This individual must be professional.

What is your present position?

Tell me a little about your present position and experience?

How long have you been in the position?

Less than 1 year (negative ☐) 2 to 5 years (reliable ☐)

Why are you looking for a new job?

Acceptable answer could be: more challenges, more responsibilities, different environment, want to work in a team environment, ability to earn more money based on effort and contribution …etc.

In this practice, the office manager will have to lead a team to make the sales objectives that are set for the practice. Can you do this and what experience do you have in leading a sales team?

Excellent ☐ Good ☐ Unprepared ☐ Ramble ☐

I have set aggressive sales objectives for the practice and it will be your job to make sure that these objectives are met and you will be compensated on your performance. Are you comfortable with this situation?

Yes ☐ Please explain ☐ No ☐

This position requires leadership abilities. Give me an example in your present position how you motivate your staff for performance?

You will also need to manage a staff of [x], including nurses. Are you able to do so? For example, if you overheard a nurse dealing with a client abruptly, how would you deal with the situation?

Excellent ☐ Good ☐ OK ☐ Poor ☐

Are you able to work without supervision to achieve your objectives? Give me an example of how you work in your present position.

Excellent ☐ Good ☐ OK ☐ Poor ☐

You are required to conduct monthly meetings and coach staff to meet sales objectives. How would you go about doing this?

Excellent ☐ Good ☐ OK ☐ Poor ☐

Give me some ideas of how you would promote the services of the practice?

Excellent ☐ Good ☐ Poor ☐

Are you able to make public presentations?

Yes ☐ No ☐ Maybe with the correct preparations ☐

What do you know about cosmetic medicine?

You want to determine if this candidate is just looking for a job or genuinely interested in this industry. The answer should show that they know something about what is required of them. Key descriptions: no elective medicine, paying patients, sales ability required, exciting environment, exceptional patient care required, patients are clients and not patients.

Excellent ☐ Good ☐ OK ☐ Not a clue ☐

What do you know about the practice?

This candidate should have researched the company thoroughly before the interview, and if they have not, then I would say that this individual is not proactive and qualified to run an aggressive cosmetic practice.

Excellent ☐ Good ☐ OK ☐ Not a clue ☐

How do you feel about people wanting cosmetic procedures?

It's the individual's choice ☐ I've not given it much thought ☐

Would you consider having cosmetic treatment done to you?

Yes ☐ No ☐ Possibly ☐ If I had the money ☐

Why should I hire you over another candidate?

A good candidate should have picked up on what you want and be able to relate your requirements with her/his skills. The answer should be something like this "Based on what you have said, you are looking for someone with these skills:...

I have all of these skills and more. In addition I can contribute in these areas:...

Auxiliary cosmetic staff

Interview questions for auxiliary cosmetic staff should follow the same format as above.

3.3 Employee's Orientation Manual

I am understating the case if I said that orienting employees to their workplaces and their jobs is one of the most neglected functions in medical practices and in general business. Countless horror stories exist about how a new employee has received a ten minute talk with the manager, and directed to his or her office position, with no further guidance or instruction. Not only is this exceedingly stressful for the employee, but it virtually guarantees a very long period of unproductiveness for the employee.

Purposes of Orientation Manual

To reduce start up cost

Proper orientation will help the new staff member get "up to speed" quickly reducing start up cost.

To reduce anxiety

Any employee, when put into a new, strange situation, will experience anxiety that can impede his or her ability to learn to do the job. Proper orientation helps to reduce anxiety that results from entering into an unknown situation, and helps provide guidelines for behaviour and conduct, so the employee doesn't have to experience the stress of guessing.

To reduce employee turnover

Employee turnover increases as employees feel they are not valued, or are put in positions where they can't possibly do their jobs. Orientation shows that the organization values the employee, and helps to provide tools necessary for succeeding in the job.

To save time for supervisors and co workers

Simply put, the better the initial orientation, the less likely supervisors and co-workers will have to spend time teaching the employee.

To develop realistic job expectations, positive attitude and job satisfaction

It is important that employees learn early on what is expected of them, and what to expect from others, in addition to learning about the values and attitudes of the organization. While people can learn from experience, they will make many mistakes that are unnecessary and potentially damaging.

Topics to be included in the Orientation Manual

Dress Code

Uniform

Most employees do not like to wear uniforms. However, in an aesthetic practice you need to maintain control of your staff's appearance. In most successful practices, there is uniformity in the staff's appearance. I prefer staff to dress with some individuality in style. For instance, your colour theme might be black and white. Individuals might choose to wear black trousers or skirts and a white shirt. I have seen beautiful black kimonos complemented with black or white slacks. Those individuals who do not like to wear slacks can wear skirts to complement the outfit. You can have the name of the practice embroidered on the back of the kimonos. Once you have decided on the theme of the outfits, you can contact a seamstress to receive a quote on the cost of making these outfits. It is very affordable. You need to put some work into it but it will pay off. Remember, your clients are evaluating everything in your practice when deciding to conduct business with you so every unique aspect of your practice will draw them closer to choosing you as their clinician for life.

Hair

Your practice focuses on aesthetics so all employees should look stylish. Obviously, hairstylists are expensive, but you might be able to negotiate with your own stylist or a nearby salon to provide a discounted service for your staff in exchange for a discount on your services. For example, a stylist might be able to style your staff's hair for a discounted rate.

Standard Rate	
Number of staff	6
Average cost of haircut	£30.00
Colour	£60.00
Number of visits/year	6
Total annual cost	£3,240.00
Your rate	
Cuts	£20.00
Colour	£40.00
Number of visits/year	6
Total cost	£2,160.00
Discount	£1,080.00

£1,080 is the annual amount of free services that you will owe the salon owner.

Muscle Relaxant treatments, dermal filler treatments, and chemical peels are some common procedures offered by non-surgical practices in exchange for discounted services. Plastic surgeons and dentists have more flexibility in this area.

Remember, the actual cost of the salon's free services is only 30% of the retail value of free services.

Benefits of Bartering

Salon

- The benefit to the salon owner is six new clients with the opportunity for referrals.

- Salons also need to market their services. This is an excellent and inexpensive way to market oneself. In chapter one, I recommended that you evaluate the clients overall appearance as part of your consultation process. For instance, if your clients need to consult with a stylist or make-up artist, the salon can be the referral source.

The Practice

- Employee's morale is heightened.

- This Perk is perceived as a benefit to your employees.

- Your staff will feel more connected to you.

- You are maintaining control of the office environment without being demanding.

- You stand a great chance of getting a number of referrals from the salon if they are pleased with the treatment results. Treat the salon owner or its employees in the same manner you would treat a client. They are a very important source of referral. Do not skimp on the product. Schedule their appointments when it is convenient for them and not for you. Engage in this type of bartering with other industries as well.

Work Ethics

The only way to determine how you want your employee to behave in your practice is to become a client yourself. Before you complete this section, visit a few businesses that are known for service-large exclusive department stores, salons and exclusive women's boutiques. Take a note-pad and write down everything that you experienced — good and bad. Write down what could have been improved. Observe ambiance, greeting, helpfulness of the staff, recommendation by the staff, music, reception desk, and enthusiasm of the staff. You need to observe at all times when you are in service industries what they do well and what could be improved. You should be aware of how your present clients are being treated in other industries in order to remain pro-active in your practice development.

Having noted your experiences elsewhere, you should draw up a checklist for your practice. The list should include the following:

- Staff must be enthusiastic and friendly.

- All staffs should be knowledgeable on procedures and be prepared to educate a client on the benefits of having aesthetic medical procedures.

- Clients should be acknowledged immediately upon entering the practice and be made to feel welcomed, regardless of how busy the practice is.

- Questions should be answered intelligently.

- Employees should not engage in personal conversation when a client is present in the practice.

- Employees should never make derogatory comments about clients.

- Client confidentiality is mandatory in this business and an employee will be fired if they divulge information on any of the practice's clients.

- Employees should never mention a client's name in front of other clients.

- On the phone, if the receptionist needs to ask personal information in the presence of another client, she should never repeat the personal information aloud.

- If the receptionist is on the phone and a client walks in, the live client is more important. She should excuse herself to the caller on the phone and greet the client in front of her, before returning to her telephone conversation.

- If you can, the waiting room should be located away from the reception desk.

Telephone Answering

If you are employing someone new for this position, you may want to hire someone with call centre experience. These individuals are client-driven and are trained in telephone sales. Your receptionist needs to be a sales person. If you are retraining an existing person, then engage him/her on some sales training course. Your office manager should look after this aspect of the business or visit us at www.kttraining.co.uk for customer service training information.

What Do Clients Want To Hear?

- A friendly voice

- So ask clients for their names and refer to them by their names.

■ People respond better and feel closer to you if you refer to them by their name. They are most likely to ask more questions and commit to a consultation.

■ Know the best possible answer to the five key questions clients will ask about any procedure.

■ Review the different Internet resource sites that your client uses and be prepared to provide intelligent answers to website's recommendations.

■ Purchase the popular health and beauty magazines, review any cosmetic related article on your business, and be prepared to answer clients' questions. Your clients need to know that you are up-to-date on everything in the industry.

■ Get the client's details and schedule an appointment.

■ Establish protocol on handling telephone inquiries: For example, should new enquiries be handed over to someone else who can take the time to answer questions?

■ The objective in a telephone inquiry is to book a consultation. You should establish some performance metric to determine how effectively inquiries are turned into appointments.

■ Do not keep clients waiting on the phone! If it cannot be avoided then investigate a system that lets the clients know the waiting time.

■ Make the telephone a marketing tool by providing clients with valuable information while they wait.

■ Develop protocols on how to respond to clients inquiries (This information should be included in your Employee's Operations Manual)

■ Develop a comprehensive web site that you can refer clients to if they require additional information. We will discuss web sites in the next chapter.

■ Provide an e-mail address which allows clients to communicate with you.

■ A dedicated person should be responsible for following up on e-mails as they occur.

Scheduling

The market survey should give you an indication of what your clients want in this area. If your practice is not 100% dedicated to cosmetic procedures, you should allocate specific times in the week or month where only cosmetic clients are booked. As the demand for more cosmetic procedures increases, you will have to allocate more days to accommodate these clients.

Remember, if you cannot work after hours or weekends, a nurse or trained office manager can pre-screen clients at these times. Furthermore, if you book a day for cosmetic clients, then do not fit in insured patients if there are free periods. Catch up on other work and leave the day just for cosmetic clients.

Reception

The front desk is a busy place and your receptionist must be trained to handle telephones and greet incoming clients with poise and ease (engage this person in training if necessary). The rules:

- Always greet the clients with a smile even if you are on the telephone.
- If on the phone, acknowledge the client, inform her how long you will be and ask her to have a seat.
- Have someone offer clients coffee, tea or water. (Pressed coffee, herbal tea, choice of sparkling or still water is preferable).
- Do not provide beverages in a plastic cup but in a nice contemporary presentation.
- Inform the clients of the waiting time.
- Provide clients with information on how long the treatment will be in case they need to adjust parking meter etc. If your practice is located in a busy downtown area with paid parking, it might be worth negotiating a discounted rate with the nearby parking facility. If the average time a patient spends in the practice is one hour, it might be wise to pay the one-hour fee. Absorb the parking cost or alternatively increase your consultation fee and your procedure fee by the cost of the parking fee. Your survey should have told you if free parking facility is a service your clients value. If it is, try your

best to negotiate a discounted fee and highlight this service in your promotional message.

■ If there are forms to complete, give these to clients and provide instructions.

Remuneration, what works best?

The annual bonus plan is the most widespread, in use by 75% of companies globally. However, only in 17% to 20% of cases will the company call it "highly effective" Most companies will say that this structured bonus system is, if anything, only "moderately" effective.

The next most popular pay programme used is the individual incentive system, which produces a higher success rate than the annual bonus program but not by much.

What makes a compensation plan work?

The definition of a successful plan is whether it meets the practice's goals and objectives.

Bottom-line objectives: A plan that helps employees to focus on the bottom line results will pay for itself through productivity, cost savings and other ways.

Top-line objectives: A plan that helps employees to focus on the top-line sales will result in increased revenue and higher profit.

Client retention objective: Plans that place emphasis on client retention will create a feeling of ownership among employees and these are usually very successful. Throughout this book, I emphasise the importance of client's acquisition and retention so your compensation plan should include some incentives to your employees for high achievement in this area.

The following sample of a Team Bonus Plan Objective Form can be used for your practice. You may follow this model for setting your objectives or create your own. It is very effective to present the results in a grid-like manner so that your team can evaluate their successes in the different areas.

Practice objective	Forecast Determine what you want to achieve for each area	Actual Evaluate your actual performance to your goals.	% to forecast	Bonus To the team
Bottom line objectives	Communication Cost Objective: eg: reduce telephone line cost by £2,000 Billing efficiency Supplies cost reduction Overtime costs reduction	Lets say that your actual result is £1500 cost reduction (set objectives for each line item and evaluate your performance to plan)	75% to target for communication cost savings.	Will be determined later
Top line objectives	Dermal fillers Botox® Chemical peels Laser hair removal Skin care Breast Aug Teeth Whitening Other services	Should be stated in your financial plan in chapter one		
Client Retention objectives	Dermal fillers Botox® Chemical peels Laser hair removal Skin care Breast Aug Teeth Whitening Other services	Should be at least 80% retention for bonus to be paid out		

Work with your accountant to determine the maximum funds available to pay out as bonuses if the three broad objectives are met.

Here is an example of how the bonuses should be distributed.

Let's say that you have 5 employees and your performance grid looks something like this:

	Segments	Results
Bottom line objective	Communication cost	75%
	Billing efficiency	82%
	Supplies cost reduction	120%
	Overtime	100%
		94.25% of target
Top line objectives	Dermal fillers Botox®	120% 150%
	Chemical peels	50%
	Laser hair removal	100%
	Skin care	92%
	Breast augmentation	98%
	Teeth whitening	120%
	Other services	100%
		103% of target
Client Retention	Dermal fillers	120%
	Botox®	120%
	Chemical peels	100%
	Laser hair removal	100%
	Skin care	100%
	Breast augmentation	100%
	Teeth whitening	70%
	Other service	70%
		97.5% of target

185

Total funds available to the team if objectives are achieved in all three segments £15,000/annually

Weighted contribution of each segment is as follows:
Bottom line contribution . 20%
Top line contribution 50%
Client retention.............. 30%

Funds available for each segment are as follows
Bottom line contribution . £3,000/year or £250/month
Top line contribution ...... £7,500/year or £625/month
Client retention.............. £4,500/year or £375/month
Total   **£15,000/year or £1,250/month.**

You have reached 98.25% of your target ((97.5 + 103 + 94.25)/3 = 98.25) so £1,228/month - is available for payout. Everyone will receive £245/month for a great team effort.

- Employees can affect results. When employees know that what they do matters, the plans have a better chance of success.

- Clear line of sight. When employees clearly see how the plan works and what brings results, the plan can work.

For those people who directly impact sales, such as the office manager and your nurses, you may want to establish an individual bonus system.

I will leave this up to you or you may contact me at yasmin@kttraining.co.uk for recommendations

Technical Training

So many practices fail to develop training and orientation processes for new and existing employees. It is assumed that employees will learn on the job. In a client-driven business such as yours there is no room for assumption. Having a procedures training manual is mandatory for any successful business to reach its objectives so take

186

the time to allocate resources for this activity. If you do not have the resources to develop a procedure manual, contact us at info@ kttraining.co.uk and we can customise a procedure manual for your practice. The cost is approximately £50 and this is a small price to pay to develop your staff's technical knowledge.

Here is an example of the set up of the treatment section of a cosmetic training manual.

Skin

[You should provide a photograph of the skin]

The skin is a large, complex organ that has many functions critical to health and survival. It consists of two primary layers, the Epidermis and the Dermis that overlay a fatty, subcutaneous tissue.

Several types of cells and specialised structures are found in the skin, which facilitate the skin's ability to regulate temperature, stimulate the immune response and monitor diverse environmental conditions (such as heat, cold, touch, etc.)

Epidermis

[You should provide a photograph of the epidermis]

The epidermis is the outermost layer of the skin and provides a relatively impermeable barrier to the penetration of liquids, irritating chemicals, and microorganisms. It can further be split into several sub layers, defined by their location and cellular shape. The deepest layer is called the basal layer; its columnar cells continually divide to produce all the rest of the cells of the epidermis. As these new cells mature, they are pushed toward the surface of the skin, accumulating the protein keratin and becoming flattened. The most superficial layer, the cornified or horny layer, consists of flat, dead, dry cells composed of keratin and little else.

Keratin

A Tough, Sulphur - containing protein that is the principal component of the epidermis, hair and nails.

Dermis

[You should provide a photograph of dermis]

The dermis, which is composed primarily of connective tissue, provides strength and elasticity to the skin and protects deeper structures from mechanical injury. The dermis is composed of two layers, which unlike the layers of the epidermis, are not clearly demarcated from each other. The thin zone immediately underneath the epidermis is the papillary dermis. The thicker, deeper layer of the dermis, extending down to the subcutaneous tissue is called the reticular dermis.

The connective tissue in the dermis consists primarily of collagen, elastin and the ground substance. Collagen fibres comprise almost 80% of the fat free, dry weight of the skin, and are responsible for its tensile strength. Elastin fibres, which have a microscopic structure similar in many ways to rubber, provide much of the flexibility of the skin. The ground substance is the matrix in which the fibres and cells of the dermis are embedded. It consists primarily of complex sugar molecules, known as glycosaminoglycans (GAGs), the two most prevalent of which are hyaluronan and chondroitin sulphate. The GAGs readily bind to water and create a viscous gel in the dermis that helps maintain the suppleness and elasticity of the skin.

Subcutaneous

[You should provide a photograph of the subcutaneous layer of the skin]

The bottom layer of skin is the subcutaneous tissue containing fat cells. These fat cells provide insulation to the body and make the skin look plump or full.

What Causes A Wrinkle?

Chronological Ageing & Wrinkles

As a person age the epidermal cells become thinner and less sticky. The thinner cells make the skin look noticeably thinner. The decreased stickiness of the cells decreases the effectiveness of the barrier function allowing moisture to be released instead of being kept in the skin. This causes dryness. The number of epidermal cells decreases by 10% per decade, and they divide more slowly as we age, making the skin less able to repair itself quickly.

The effects of aging on the dermal layer are significant. Not only does the dermal layer thin, but also less collagen is produced, and the elastin fibres that provide elasticity wear out. These changes in the scaffolding of the skin cause the skin to wrinkle and sag. Also, sebaceous glands get bigger but produce less sebum, and the number of sweat glands decreases. Both changes lead to skin dryness.

The rete-ridges of the dermal-epidermal junction flatten out, making the skin more fragile and making it easier for the skin to shear. This process also decreases the amount of nutrients available to the epidermis by decreasing the surface area in contact with the dermis, also interfering with the skin's normal repair process.

In the subcutaneous layer, the fat cells get smaller with age. This leads to more noticeable wrinkles and sagging, as the fat cells cannot "fill in" the damage from the other layers.

Cosmetic Procedures

You can't reverse the flow of time and become younger. However, with the wide array of rejuvenating treatments available today, you can slow down many of the effects of ageing and photo ageing. You can't become younger, but you can look younger and appear more attractive by working with (Your name Clinic) to choose the skin rejuvenation treatment that is right for you.

This segment of your training manual provides a description and discussion of the scope of treatments available from the (Your name Clinic) for skin and facial rejuvenation.

Treatments discussed in this segment:

- Microdermabrasion
- Chemical peels
- Muscle Relaxant injections

- Dermal fillers
- Skin care
- IPL

Microdermabrasion Procedures:

What is microdermabrasion?

It is a skin resurfacing procedure used in addition to chemical peels, dermabrasion and laser resurfacing. This procedure was pioneered in Europe 10 years ago.

What is the procedure?

The clinician uses a hand-piece connected to a system, which disperses an abrasive substance (usually aluminium oxide) in crystalline form. This abrasive substance is pulled from a reservoir, passes through the hand-piece and passes back and forth on the skin, abrading it without heat. The used abrasive material and dead skin are vacuumed into a repository for easy removal. Layers of the epidermis are removed which result in a younger, fresher looking skin.

How much penetration is possible?

The depth of treatment is determined by the speed of movement of the hand-piece against the skin. The slower the passes the deeper the results.

What should the client experience after treatment?

The client's skin may feel tight as if it had been exposed to sun or wind. The skin may peel and should be well moisturised with proper products and a strong sunscreen, preferably 15 SPF or higher. Some clients may develop slight redness and swelling, especially after a deeper treatment level during the removal of blemished or thicker skin. Erythema or a slight redness will occur from a few hours to a few days depending on the skin's sensitivity. It is possible some peeling may last for one or two days.

What are some indications for treatment of microdermabrasion and how does it benefit the clients?

Anyone can have microdermabrasion including men and teenagers. Microdermabrasion polishes, softens and reduces fine lines on the face shown through facial expressions. Areas most concerned with fine lines and wrinkles are cheeks, forehead and around the mouth. Treatments will smooth pigment changes like brown spots, pigmentation and melanosis. Acne skin is exfoliated with suctioning, unclogging pores and leaving the skin refreshed. Acne scars usually require 10 initial treatment visits to achieve visible improvement. Microdermabrasion enhances poor, dull, congested or thickened skin by gently resurfacing the superficial skin layers.

Sales Preparation

What is microdermabrasion?

Answer: Microdermabrasion is a skin rejuvenating procedure used to refine and revitalise the skin. This procedure is ideal for everyone since it makes the skin more youthful looking by refining the pores, improving the texture of the skin and exfoliation of the skin.

How is it done?

Answer: The clinician uses a hand piece, which disperses (aluminium, other substances etc.) on the face. This crystalline substance is used to abrade the skin without heat thus it is less invasive than laser with less down-time for you. In fact, you can have it in your lunch hour. You will need a series of treatments to see the actual effects of the treatment.

How will I look after the procedure?

Answer: Your skin may feel tight as if it had been exposed to sun or wind. You may peel but this is only noticeable to you. It is possible to develop slight redness and swelling, especially after deeper treatment. The result is worth the slight discomfort. Your skin will have a healthier glow and this treatment will complement any other cosmetic treatment of the face.

How much does it cost?

Answer: We offer the series of treatments for [xxxx] since it is best that you have a series of treatments to see the maximum result. If you wish to have only one treatment, the price is [xxxx].

Follow this same format for the other procedures that you offer in the practice.

The manuals are available for sale through our retail division. E-mail or call us for more information on our training resources.

Dentists/Surgeons/Other Specialties

Dentists

A procedure manual should be developed by the principal/manager on the basics of dentistry and what the practice is trying to achieve. A simple description of the practice's services and how these services benefit the patients should be included. A section should be dedicated to selling these services against competitive procedures and services. You may wish to follow the microdermabrasion outline.

Surgeons

Your procedure manual should consist of a description of the practice's goals and ways the practice differs from its competitors. A brief description of your surgical procedures. You will want to describe how your surgical skill differs from your competitors and why patients should choose your practice over your competitors or the large national groups. Your employees need to know this information.

 Your Employee Orientation Manual should include the following:

- Dress Code (uniform, hair, make-up...etc)
- Work Ethics (lateness, attitude, sick leave, time away from work

- Clear guidelines of each person's responsibilities
- Telephone answering protocols
- Scheduling protocols
- Reception protocols
- Bonus Program
- Employee evaluation protocols
- Human Resource issues

Your Procedure Manual should include the following:

Dentistry and Facial Aesthetics

Two separate sections (dentistry and facial aesthetics) follow a similar guideline to the microdermabrasion brief.

Plastic Surgeons

Two separate sections consisting of surgical procedures and non-surgical procedures

Non Surgical Specialists

Follow the Microdermabrasion example above.

Chapter 4

Internal Operations

Expense reporting procedures... Time recording procedures... Where the paper is kept... Where the snacks are kept... What to do if the copier is broken... What type of medical software should we choose Benefits scheme... Sick leave... Holiday scheduling... The list could go on forever.

These aren't the things that make or break a business. However, they should be worked out and communicated to your staff in order to keep your costs down, make the workplace workable, and enhance the efficiency of your employees. I have already discussed the orientation manual in chapter three. The systems and processes discussed in this chapter should be included in your orientation manual under the appropriate heading.

As changes occur at your practice employees will need to know, and they'll naturally have questions. Sometimes they just want answers, and sometimes they need reassurance. Most often, different groups of employees need different levels of communication during times of transition from traditional medicine to aesthetic medicine. For example, if a client calls to complain about the outcome of a certain procedure, you need to have clear guidelines on how the complaint should be managed.

Employees also need communications about periodic and routine events that affect them such as performance reviews, annual pay raises and so on.

The smallest of cosmetic practice will need an operation manual to ensure that the practice is operating efficiently at all times.

In larger practices this work can be delegated to the office manager, but if you are a small operation without an office manager you may want to out-source the development of your internal operations manual or you may have your manual customized for you by K-T Training. For more information on our services, e-mail us at info@ kttraining.co.uk.

In this section of the book, I will discuss the systems and processes for five key areas of the business.

- Dealing with Web and Telephone Enquiries
- Telephone Protocols
- Pre-Consultation Protocol
- Consultation Protocol
- Conducting Effective Management Meetings

Revenue Pathway

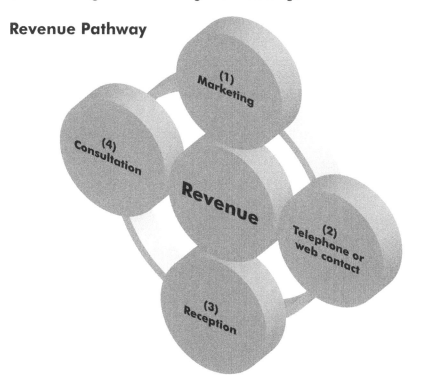

Marketing is not a magical activity that creates practice revenue without the practice's direct involvement. All employees, and most importantly, the practice owners/practice managers need to understand how a private practice earns its revenue.

The marketing activities described in chapter 1, section1.6 listed a range of activities the practice will undertake to attract patients into the clinic. Marketing does not stop here, it is a continuous process. Once the potential client decides to contact the clinic, the following activities must be recorded.

4.1 Telephone and Web Enquiry Protocol

Call Logging Sheets

Call Logging Sheet for New Enquiries: if the practice does not have a contact management system, it is recommended that a call logging sheet be developed as follows:

Name of Caller
Contact Number:
Details of the call: Botox inquiry etc.....
How did the caller find out about the clinic: web-advertisement-referral-salon-yellow pages- etc....
Activity relating to call: consultation booked-info mailed out-e-mail sent to caller
Date to follow-up
Response to follow-up
Employee who took call-
Employee to follow-up on call
Results:

Set up a binder with weekly and monthly inserts.
File the information appropriately.

Web enquiries should be logged and details of the activities carried out to confirm the consultation.

Name of web enquiry
Contact Number: e-mail address
Details of the enquiry: Botox inquiry etc…..
Activity relating to inquiry: consultation booked-info mailed out-e-mail sent to caller
Date to follow-up
Response to follow-up
Employee who responded to e-mail
Employee to follow-up on e-mail
Results:

Managers should review the information weekly as part of their responsibilities to assess the staff's ability to convert enquiries into booked consultations. Practice owners and managers should discuss ways to improve inefficiencies if they exit. In almost all cases, inefficiencies will exist. A CRM System can track this type of information and provide detail reports on enquiry management. Please note, a CRM System and the call logging sheet only reports information which identifies clinic inefficiencies. If the manager or clinic owner does not implement changes to rectify inefficiencies, the effort it takes to gather this information is useless. I have observed that most clinics are unaware of how inefficient they are, since there is no established protocol to evaluate communication inefficiencies.

The Computer

In the previous chapter, we recommended that you set practice goals. It is difficult to track pre-set goals without the use of a computer. You will need to find a good software program to allow you to track the marketing goals of the entire practice and to collect information and data that accurately represent your practice. For example, the average age of your clients, which services they prefer, which services generate the most profit, the sales revenue generated for each business unit, your consultation closing ratio, clients' follow-up records, response rates from advertising campaigns, and identifying new services to include in your product portfolio.

This information is vital in developing your long-term marketing and growth strategies. The information will determine where to focus your effort and resources to generate new clients and keep your present clients returning to the practice. Presently, I do not know of any medical software with these capabilities. We have found one CRM software which can be customized to record marketing information in a medical practice. The name of the software is ACT. ACT is not a medical software and the diary can only accommodate one clinic which is inconvenient for large practices. However, one can run this software parallel to a normal medical software where clients are booked and scheduled for appointments. The marketing information can be recorded in ACT. Therefore, at the end of the day, all sales and marketing data must be entered into the ACT software for reporting purposes.

If you do have a system that can record customer information, then begin to record all details relating to the customer as follows:

Codes should be established to record customer status

Code	New Customer	Existing Customer
Botox	NB	EB
Dermal Filler	NDF	EDF
Radiesse	NRAD	ERAD
AHA Peels	NAHP	EAHP
TCA	NTCP	ETCP
Laser Hair Removal	NLR	ELR
Skin Care	NSC	ESC

Every sale must be coded to identify the sale type.

A report on revenue generation and by types of customer is necessary to evaluate if the practice is on track to forecast and if the business is managed for long term success. Qualitative and quantitative reports are necessary to run the business successfully. You simply cannot evaluate the business if you have only financial information. You need qualitative information to measure staff's and manager's performance. A manager needs to manage the practice to achieve the practice's long and short term goals. Therefore, managing staff to complete daily tasks is not enough in a marketing focused practice. If you recall in chapter one, I demonstrated the power of repeat customers. The same information is presented below.

Dermal Filler Projection- Year 2

	Jan	Feb	Mar	Apr	May	Jun	Jul	Aug	Sept	Oct	Nov	Dec
New Patients	5	5	5	5	5	5	5	5	5	5	5	5
Previous year Patients												
Jan-Jun	5	5	5	5	5	5	5	5	5	5	5	5
Jul-Aug	5	5	5	5	5	5	5	5	5	5	5	5
Present Year Patients												
Jan-Jun							5	5	5	5	5	5
Total	15	15	15	15	15	15	20	20	20	20	20	20
Total Year 2 Revenue = 210 treatments at £275/treatment = £57,750												

For example, the report for year two dermal filler actual should read as follows:

> Dermal Filler Total Revenue for Year Two: £57,750
>
> New Dermal Filler Clients (NDF)   60
>
> Existing Dermal Filler Clients (EDF)   150
>
> This is the ratio that you are looking for in a relationship business.

For example, if year two performance actual reads as follows:

> Dermal Filler Total Revenue for Year Two: £57,750
>
> New Dermal Filler Clients (NDF)   120
>
> Existing Dermal Filler Clients (EDF)   90
>
> This situation is an indication of long term problems

As the practice owner, I will be pleased to see that the practice has achieved its practice goals and the new business has over-exceeded its forecast, but I will be equally concerned as to why 60 existing patients had not returned for repeat procedures. An automated system will measure your repeat business. If repeat client's objectives were not achieved, I would quickly follow up and create an enticement to get these clients back into the clinic. Quick response to inefficiencies will minimize future financial risks.

Telephone Protocol

Below is an example of how a telephone call should be handled

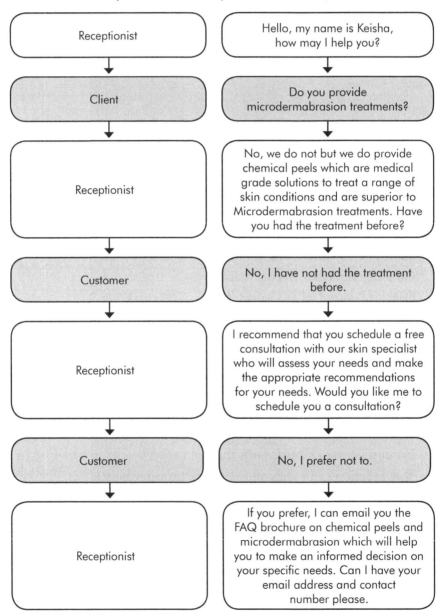

The receptionist objective for every enquiry is to schedule a consultation with the clinician. Therefore, the call has to be managed effectively to achieve the outcome. In this case, the receptionist is not successful in booking the consultation, however, if the FAQ brochure provides information on the benefits of chemical peels and its advantage over Microdermabrasion, the receptionist has a good chance of solidifying the consultation at a later date. My company does this on a daily basis when doctors call in to enquire about our training. In most cases, we win the deal because we have developed communication pieces that explain the advantages of choosing our company over the hundreds of training companies that exist.

4.2 Consultation Protocol

The marketing process and the models used for predicting consumer decision-making are very complex and much too involved for this book. However, the information presented below will give you some insight into the decision-making process that a consumer goes through before making any buying decision. I use this information to make recommendations to you on your communication with the client when conducting a consultation. The information presented below was taken from an Internet site **"Tutor2u.com"**. This site is an excellent source of information on a diverse range of marketing subjects. I recommend that you visit the site for more in-depth reading on consumer and marketing issues.

Buyer Behaviour

The decision-making process

How do clients buy? Research suggests that clients go through the following five-stage decision-making process in any purchase.

Needs recognition and problem awareness: New cosmetic clients have passed this stage before they come in contact with your practice. However, new and existing clients will have additional needs, and hopefully they will look only to your practice for the solution.

Information search: Most of today's aesthetic clients have done their research before they meet you. Your promotional efforts should be focused enough to pull potential clients to your clinic. By now you should have determined your target market and your communication message should be designed to make clients want to call you.

Evaluation of alternatives: This is the stage that most clients will come in contact with your practice. If your office team has been fully trained, they will be very effective in moving the client to the consultation stage. Your staff needs to be trained on customer service skills, developing rapport on the phone, and selling skills. These skill sets will dramatically improve their effectiveness on the phone and in person.

Purchase: The client commits to a consultation with you. If effective in your consultation, you will get a commitment during the consultation for non surgical treatment or surgery.

Post–purchase evaluation: This is the stage that most practices fail. Once clients have made the decision to let you provide their treatment, it does not mean that they are satisfied. Follow-up is absolutely critical to alleviate any post-purchase remorse. Remember repeat clients will sustain your long-term growth. For dentists and surgeons promoting high priced procedures, the follow-up protocol is necessary to make sure the client does not change his/her mind. Follow-up is necessary to determine if the client has any concerns about the proposed treatment or the treatment they have received. Medical practices demonstrate weaknesses in many areas of management but this area is especially weak. Eighty percent of clients will not complain but switch providers.

This model is important for anyone making marketing decisions. It forces the practice to consider the whole buying process rather than just the purchase decision (when it may be too late for a business to influence the choice!).

The model implies that clients pass through all stages in every purchase. However, in more routine purchases, clients often skip or reverse some of the stages.

For example, a student buying a favourite hamburger would recognise the need (hunger) and go right to the purchase decision, skipping the information search and evaluation. However, the model is very useful when it comes to understanding any purchase that requires some thought and deliberation.

The buying process starts with need recognition. At this stage, the buyer recognises a problem or need (e.g. I am hungry, we need a new sofa, I have a headache) or responds to a marketing stimulus (e.g. you pass Starbucks and are attracted by the aroma of coffee and chocolate muffins).

An 'aroused' client then needs to decide how much information (if any) is required. If the need is strong and there is a product or service that meets the need close to hand, then a purchase decision is likely to be made there and then. If not, then the process of information search begins.

A client can obtain information from several sources:

■ Personal sources: family, friends, neighbours, etc

■ Commercial sources: web, advertising, salespeople, retailers, dealers, packaging, point-of-sale displays

The usefulness and influence of these sources of information will vary by product and by client. Research suggests that customers' value and respect personal sources more than commercial sources (the influence of 'word of mouth'). The challenge for the practice is to identify which information sources are most influential in their target markets. In aesthetic medicine, word of mouth, web optimization, and referrals are the best sources of influence. We will discuss this issue in your promotional activities.

How does the client use the information obtained?

An important determinant of the extent of evaluation is whether the client feels 'involved' in the product. By involvement, we mean the degree of perceived relevance and personal importance that accompanies the choice.

Where a purchase is 'highly involving', the client is likely to carry out extensive evaluation. High-involvement purchases include those involving high expenditure or personal risk — for example, buying a house, a car or making investments... and the choice to have cosmetic enhancement procedures. Low involvement purchases (e.g. buying a soft drink, choosing some breakfast cereals in the supermarket) have very simple evaluation processes.

Why should an aesthetic practice need to understand the client evaluation process? The answer lies in the kind of information that the practice's marketing team needs to provide clients in different buying situations.

In high-involvement decisions, the marketer needs to provide a good deal of information about the positive consequences of buying. You and your employees will need to stress the important attributes of the practice and your superiority over the competition. You need to know your strengths over the competition. You should mystery shop some of your competitors to evaluate their strengths and weaknesses.

Post-purchase evaluation — cognitive dissonance

The final stage is the post-purchase evaluation of the decision. It is common for clients to experience concerns after making a purchase decision. This arises from a concept that is known as 'cognitive dissonance'. The client, having had the procedure, may feel that the result is not as expected. At least 50% of cosmetic clients go through this stage and unless your patient care pathway includes a post-treatment follow-up with your clients, you have no way of finding out how they feel. In these circumstances your client will not return immediately, may choose not to repeat the procedure at all or is likely to switch to another practice.

Recommendation on ways to improve the Consultation Process

Evaluation Stage (stage that client will begin to make contact with clinics)

The decision to have surgical or non-surgical treatment is a high involvement decision and at the evaluation stage, the patient is still concerned about the risks involved. Their concerns can be summarised as follows:

Functional: risk that the treatment will not work.

Telephone call-receptionist must focus on clinician's expertise, and safety of products.

In person: Manufacturer information, clinical papers, before and after photographs, referral list, staff that has been treated with the procedure in question, your credentials and educational information on the safety of the product will minimise this concern.

Financial: risk that the treatment will not be worth the cost. A client will feel this way if an inappropriate recommendation was made, the physician reacted to the patient request without defining the client's needs, and the treatment outcome is poor. When providing your first treatment to the client, you need to concentrate less on the profitability of the procedure and more on making the client happy.

Time: risk that the time spent researching and having the treatment will be wasted if the result does not meet expectations. Thorough assessment of the client's needs and setting realistic expectations will minimise this concern.

Social: risk that the treatment will cause embarrassment before others. Before and after photographs, names of satisfied clients and effective communication with the client will make the client feel at ease.

Pre-consultation Recommendations

You should delegate the pre-consultation responsibilities to a trained staff member. This is an essential part of building up the relationship with your client and should include:

- Observation of the client's body language. If the client is nervous, your staff should calm him or her down by finding out what concerns they have. Deal with this issue first before moving on to the pre-consultation protocol. It might be useful to discuss the clinician's credentials. Any article on the clinician's success as a cosmetic clinician is helpful here. Make sure that all concerns are addressed before you move on. At the evaluation stage, 95% of clients are concerned about one of the five risks. If you and your staff are prepared, you will have no problem moving the client to the purchase stage.

- Help the client to define their perceived problem and aesthetic needs.

- Once her/his needs are established, determine expectations.

- Explain all the possible alternatives and treatment outcomes, answering questions on safety and outcome. Provide before and after photographs of existing satisfied clients.

- If the client requests a personal recommendation, ask if a staff member is adequate, or whether they need an outside source. Have a number of recommendation letters from satisfied clients available for this purpose. If the client wants to speak directly to another client, provide names of past clients who have had the treatment. You need to ask some of your regular clients if they mind being a testimonial resource. You may want to give them some type of discount for the inconvenience.

- Review the clinician's credentials and success record. Show before and after photographs of other clients' results. Review the clinic's dossier.

Consultation with the Clinician

Before any cosmetic consultation, make improvements on your listening skills.

- Actively listen to the clients and make eye contact at all times.

- Do not just listen, but make sure that you hear the client and rephrase what is being said to ensure clarity.

- Pay particular attention to non-verbal clues, such as posture or fidgeting.

- Speak clearly and directly to the client.

- Encourage the client to express his or her self without being judged.

- No matter how busy you are, make the client feel that you are unhurried and have all the time for her/him.

- Do not stand when speaking to the clients. This is considered an authoritarian pose.

- Ask if there are other concerns. This approach gives the clients the opportunity to express their anxieties.

- Key questions to ask are: What is your key concern? What do you expect to achieve from the treatment? How much are you willing to spend at this time?

- Give your recommendations on the best treatment options-surgical and non surgical.

It is best to delegate fee discussions to your practice manager or pre-consultation specialist, but if you are handling this responsibility be very strategic when the issue of cost is discussed. I have found that when it comes to the cost of cosmetic procedures, cosmetic clients seem to think that the cost is too high regardless of the amount. Client's perception of value for medical aesthetic treatments is out of line. It can be that patients have received medical services for free and still look at medical aesthetic treatments as medical treatments and not as a commercial high end service.

The way I deal with this subject is by breaking down the cost into smaller increments. For example: the average cost for breast augmentation is £4,000. The benefits derived from having the procedure will last for at least 10 years before the patient may need to repeat the procedure. The cost to the client is £400/year to enjoy the pleasure of having fuller breasts, improving her physical appearance and improving her self-confidence. Even if the client has to finance this procedure, the cost of the procedure spread out over its minimum lifetime period is less than what the same client will pay to have her hair coloured and styled.

Most women spend more anually on eating out, entertainment, hair, nails, spas and clothing than they will spend on cosmetic procedures. Do not compromise on your fee. It is fair. Clients need to understand that the investment they are making in plastic surgery/non surgical medicine is like investing in a house or car. The benefits extend over a long period of time and the cost should be assessed over the lifetime of the procedure. The same goes for high end dentistry work.

Ask if the client wants to go ahead with the recommended treatment at this time. If you are injecting dermal fillers or botulinum toxin you should be very liberal with products on the first treatment. Focus on the lifetime value of the patient to the practice and not on your immediate profit potential from this procedure. Compromise on your profit and provide excellent treatment.

- Take before and after photographs!

- Invest in a comfortable and modern treatment chair.

- Make sure that the lightning in the room is soft and appropriate for the types of treatment offered.

- Make sure that the client is pleased with the result.

- This piece of advice might seem juvenile but many top injectors invest in expensive hand-held mirrors. All mirrors in the practice (even in the bathroom) should be of excellent quality. The lightening in the room should be soft.

- Post-treatment care should be provided on a laminated purse-size card. Make sure that a contact number is listed in case of emergencies.

- If you do not have an aesthetician in your practice then purchase some cover-up makeup in different skin tones and a variety of lipsticks for your clients to use after their treatment. Most clients will bring their own, but it is nice to provide this service.

- Follow up! Follow up! Follow up on first-time clients. It will pay off.

- Remember: If you do not feel a particular treatment is appropriate for a client, don't do it.

Meetings

If there is going to be a meeting, there needs to be a reason for it. If there is no reason, the meeting should not take place. The main reasons for staff to hold meetings include information sharing, information processing and problem solving. Information sharing may, for example, be necessary if the practice has decided to extend the office hours. Often this type of information can be communicated by memos, but in a small office it is nice to meet with everyone to involve them in the decision-making process. Another example may be that the practice decides to include a new procedure in its portfolio. Staff will need to gather information on the procedure and discuss how this change will impact their responsibilities. Problem solving may be a case where the employees need to get together to discuss ways to improve a particular problem. For example, client retention objectives are not being reached.

For whatever reason you meet, here are the steps in conducting an effective staff meeting.

Agenda

- Create an agenda based on the purpose of the meeting.
- Get feedback from staff members on the content of the meeting.
- Distribute the agenda in advance so that staff members are prepared with comments and ideas.
- Know what you want to achieve in the meeting.
- Explain to everyone what you intend to achieve in the meeting.
- Ask others what they want to achieve in the meeting.
- List yours and the staff's objectives on a flip chart and paste the page on the wall so that everyone can see what the objectives are.
- Have someone in the team take minutes of the meeting.
- Start with the most important item on the agenda and allocate a certain amount of time for each topic.
- To make the meeting run smoothly, there should be a facilitator, a timekeeper and a note-taker.

The facilitator provides focus on the topic at hand and will encourage communication among the group. The timekeeper will keep track of the time slots given for each topic on the agenda. The note-taker will record notes on the flip chart.

- At the end of the meeting, review the objectives and make sure that everyone is happy with the outcome of the meeting.
- Follow-up. Distribute the typed minutes of the meeting to the appropriate personnel within the day.

■ Implement recommendations and suggestions.

Following these steps will allow for more effective meetings with your staff and increase morale when staff sees that the practice owner is willing to involve and share information with everyone in the practice.

If the practice does not hold regular meetings, I recommend you hold at least one monthly meeting to review progress in achieving your sales objectives.

Monthly Progress Review Meeting Format

Have someone take the minutes of the meeting. Review reports on the following:

■ New clients for each business unit/to pre-set goals

■ Clients retention/to goal

■ Sales revenue for different business units/ to pre-set goal

■ Consultation closing ratio/to goal

■ Result on follow up calls

■ Results on promotional advertising

■ Result on cross selling initiatives

■ New business opportunities

If you have achieved your planned goal in each area congratulation should be handed out to the team. Consider whether you need to set higher goals.

Use your graph to demonstrate the bonus calculation and pay out bonuses. Then use your graph to demonstrate the new monthly objectives.

Thank everyone for his or her contribution.

If you have not achieved monthly goals, identify areas for improvement. Delegate the responsibilities for making sure recommendations are implemented to an appropriate member of staff. Some of the areas that your staff may need retraining on to achieve the practice's objectives are:

- Relationship selling
- Communication skills
- Telephone answering skills
- Questioning skills
- Stress management
- Handling objections
- Cross selling related procedures

Have your manager source outreach programs to help your staff improve their skill sets or visit our website at www.kttraining.co.uk for more information on personal development training.

The information covered in this chapter should be included in the Staff's Operational Manual. These are systems and processes which your employees need to be aware of. The practice manager and business owner need to create and develop this type of structure to effectively grow the business. A well organized business will outperform a disorganized business in the long term. It does not matter if the disorganized business is generating more revenue at the moment. Sooner or later an inefficient practice will experience difficulty as the market becomes more saturated.

"If you fail to plan Your plan to fail"

Chapter 5

Internal and External Promotions

Everything that we have spoken about so far involves the discipline of marketing. I have placed the subject of promotion as the last topic to discuss for a reason. If you have not made the necessary improvements described in previous chapters, I believe that any promotional campaign will generate poor return on your investment. I will give you a real life example, which occurred with a client of mine. An advertisement was placed in Tattler magazine; the response was excellent, resulting in an influx of incoming calls from readers. However, the receptionist was unaware that the advertisement had been placed. No protocol was established on how to handle the extra calls. The receptionist was not trained to answer clients' inquiries, she was not advised on scheduling procedures for the excess demand, and most importantly clients were placed on hold for a long time.

If you are going to advertise or engage in any promotional activity, call a meeting to involve staff in the decision and work out the logistics for how the incoming calls are going to be handled. Review scheduling changes. Make sure everyone is prepared for the influx of new clients and relate the extra work to the bonus potential. Overall, it is useless to participate in any promotional campaign if you are not properly trained in the procedure, you have not established pre-and post consultation protocols, your employees are not properly trained and your consultation-closing ratio is low.

Promotional Activities

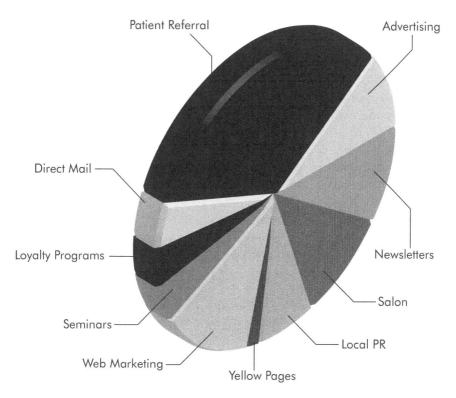

The charts above represent a healthy promotional mix for established and new businesses. Presently most large clinics and independent clinicians rely too heavily on just advertising for exposure. As the market becomes more competitive and there are more suppliers using advertising as their sole promotional activity, the impact of advertising will lose its effectiveness. Therefore, it is important that new and established businesses focus on a broader range of activities to generate market awareness for their services. Below are various promotional activities which should be added to your promotional mix. The recommendations are segmented by internal and external promotion.

5.1 Internal Promotion

Your old database

According to Mr J Yanik Silver (an expert in practice marketing for the American market) your most profitable assets are your current and former patients. Most doctors don't realise this. In many instances physicians who enter the aesthetic market are too busy trying to get new clients instead of paying attention to the patients they already have. If your present patient base is similar to the demographics we discussed in chapter one, you are sitting on a gold mine. Your patients trust you; they have faith in you, they come to see you regularly, and hopefully they like you. It would make sense to become somewhat assertive in promoting your new services to your existing patient base. Most physicians have thousands of old patient files stored away. Now is the time to bring them back into your practice. You already know that 90% of patients who opt for cosmetic procedures are female. You know that over 60% of all cosmetic procedures done in 2006 were to male and females in the age range of 19–50.

Go to your files and pull out all the female patients between the ages of 19 and 50. Pull out at least a thousand patients that fit these criteria. Choose patients by profession and income level. Now you are ready to do some work.

After you have completed your list of hot prospects, send a personal letter to activate interest for your new services. Your letter needs to show concern for your patients' well-being and also an irresistible inducement to come back. The best inducement is a free service or product. Everybody loves to get something for free.

Free is the best offer you can make. Use something with a high-perceived value but very little hard cost to you. A free chemical peel or some kind of skin care product works very nicely. The cost of providing a free chemical peel is very low, especially if the doctor/dentist can delegate the responsibilities to a nurse or assistant. In the long run, providing this free service to existing patients to pull them back into your practice is much cheaper than the cost of promotional activities aimed at attracting new clients into the practice. Once your old patients return, you will get these patients back into the habit of using your other services, especially if, at the same time, you promote special offers for other services they may be interested in.

A smart thing to do is set an expiry date and limit the time for these free services. This way you have a very structured offer. You may want to structure promotional offers during slow periods which usually occur in the summer and at the beginning of the year.

Below are examples of a promotional piece

Notice both advertisements state the benefit of the single treatment in bold. Both advertisements focus on the 30-55 target market since the advertisement lists specific problems related to this target market. In the Muscle Relaxant Advertisement, there is a call to action statement with an expiry date. The peel advertisement gives the target audience an option to book a consultation or to attend the regular seminars for more information. These mock-ups hopefully are examples which can be used to design your other promotional pieces.

Make your Clients Ambassadors of your clinic

Simply providing excellent work will not get you dozens of referrals coming through the door. You have to ask your clients for referrals, and I suggest that you develop a referral program if you are allowed to do so in your country.

Print a number of referral cards for the practice, using a style that is in keeping with your other promotional material. The back of the card should state the following:

Presented to :_____

Referred By:_____

Date:_____

Give these out to clients who you believe will generate referrals. Your present client will give the cards out to associates and friends who may need your services. These cards are presented to the practice when the new client books a consultation and will be used to track referral source. The rewards for clients introducing non-invasive treatment referrals will be different from the rewards offered for surgical referrals, and it is for the clinician, surgeon or practice manager to determine the amount of compensation for each referral. It must be meaningful because people will lose interest if the target is unrealistic and the rewards are unattractive.

Five non-invasive treatment referrals within the price range of £60 to £300, is worth a £100 gift certificate towards any treatment offered in the practice. A £100 gift certificate will cost the clinic little in direct cost and is far less expensive than using advertising to attract 5 new clients into the practice. Ninety percent of referred clients will elect to have a procedure. New patients generated through advertising are still in the evaluation mode and in 50% of the cases; they will want to think about going ahead with the procedure after the consultation is completed. If the client provides 5 surgical referrals that elect to go ahead with the surgery, a £700 gift certificate of services might be more appropriate. You could also offer free non-invasive procedures for surgical referrals.

At the end of the month review the number of referrals generated by the program and send out gift certificates with a thank-you letter to all your clients who participated in the program. If you need more help in designing your direct mail campaign, contact our office for information on our direct mail services.

Make the Waiting Room a Soft Sell Environment

It never ceases to amaze me how many physicians ignore the aesthetics of their office environment. Your image via the media, direct mail, postcards, newsletters, brochures, stationery, office layout, furniture, staff's appearance, and staff's demeanour over the telephone and in person are vital elements that stimulate positive or negative recommendations. First impressions do count so make an effort to improve the office environment.

Here Are Some Recommendations

- Position the waiting-room away from the reception desk.
- Provide a plasma screen television with information on new innovations in the industry.
- It goes without saying that the office environment should be aesthetically pleasing. Hire a designer if necessary.

- Have an expensive leather binder with unlimited reference letters from happy patients.

- Have a computer workstation available for clients who may want to work while waiting to see you.

- Review monthly fashion magazines and file positive articles on any procedure you offer in a leather binder which should be displayed in the waiting area.

- If the doctor has had positive reviews from journalists, make sure they are displayed in the waiting room.

- If you are introducing a new procedure, make sure it is highlighted in the waiting room. Do not crowd the waiting room with a lot of advertisements. Employ very discrete promotion in the waiting room. If you bombard the area with ads, then the chance of a client reacting to any ad is slim. However, if you present new and existing treatments skill-fully in the practice, it will grab the client's interest. The attention clue is when the client asks you "what is this all about?" and "does it work?"

Bingo! You have their interest and you can work through the five decision-making processes in one go. This is the easiest way to cross-sell new treatments.

Practice Newsletter on New & Existing Procedures

Newsletters are a great way of soft-selling new treatments without appearing too aggressive. A well-written newsletter is educational and informative and keeps the lines of communication open. Your newsletter should be exactly as it sounds — a letter filled with news!

Do not commercialise. Report the latest developments taking place in your field, and explain how your practice has applied such developments to improve it's services to it's clients. Repeat procedures that require follow-up treatments such as a new laser hair removal system are excellent services to promote in a newsletter. A new surgical technique that reduces down-time is also news to patients. Education on liposuction, facelifts, nose reshaping, buttock lifts and cheek implants are areas of interest to the aesthetic market. I am amazed how many people are still in the dark about breast implants, so here is your chance to put their fears at ease.

On the last page of your newsletter you may want to include a tear off gift certificate for £20 towards any non-surgical procedures. Make sure there is an expiry date attached to the certificate. Expiry dates usually force clients to act immediately.

Think creatively about where to distribute your newsletters. Beside your clients, distribute your newsletters to hair salons, beauty salons, gyms ,and your local country club etc.
For more information on developing and designing your personal newsletter, contact:
K-T Training or K-T Solutions at info@kttraining.co.uk.

Frequent User Program for Existing Patients

Patients who use a lot of the practice's services should be rewarded for their loyalty. A frequent user program is a sure-fire way to keep satisfied clients returning to the practice. An example of a successful frequent user program is one where patients who spend over £2000/ annually on cosmetic services will receive a series of chemical peels or a certain number of laser hair removal treatments for free. The costs of these treatments are inexpensive, and they can be carried out by the nurse or your staff members. The discount is small but the perceived value to the client is great. Make yourself standout by letting your customers know that you recognise their contribution to your business and thank them for their patronage. This type of activity demonstrates the true essence of customer service. You are thanking your customer for their business by offering them something for free. It rarely happens to me but when it does, it feels great.

Promoting Your Business on the Internet

Promoting your business on the Internet provides more than just advertising value; it can also automate repetitive tasks and enable potential clients to assess your practice before they have made an appointment with you.

A well designed and informative website is essential as this can create the first impression of your business, which can be a decisive factor for your potential client when choosing your services.

When users surf the Internet searching for your services, they need to be directed to your site, not your competitor's site. This can be achieved very cost effectively by optimising Internet tools. Remember that e-mail is a very low-cost method of communicating with people, and allows you to communicate across the world and around the clock.

The importance of your web presence

Communicating business information: Inform clients about your hours of operation, what you do, how to contact you, methods of payment and your location.

Establish a presence in the marketplace: Pass out your business card to thousands, perhaps millions, of potential clients

Reach your desired market: The majority of Internet users either are - or will be - professionals with disposable income.

Serve your clients: Allow clients to browse catalogues, make enquiries, and gain information on treatments.

Reach the media: List public relations material.

Test new products and treatments: With a web page you can ask for and receive feedback. Use a questionnaire to get information about treatments, new product results and amenities

Sell products and treatments: Clients can make appointments and book treatments directly through their personal computers.

Open international markets: With a simple page on the World Wide Web, you can communicate with international markets as easily as with the company across the street.

Offer a 24-hour service: The Internet serves users 24 hours a day, seven days a week, with no long-distance charges and minimal overheads.

Web Site Design

Websites can only promote your business effectively if they are well designed and well constructed. Think carefully about the content you want to include on your website well before you start designing or commissioning a web designer. The sort of information you might think of putting on the web will include:

- E-mail link

- Online brochure and product range

- List of treatments

- Procedure description

- Glossary of terms

- FAQ (frequently asked questions)

- Pre- and post-procedure photographs

- Information about the practice (facilities, opening hours, etc)

- Location and map links

- Links to sites with related information

- Testimonials from current clients

- Staff qualifications, accreditations and photographs

- News and events (seminars, etc)

If you have an existing colour scheme or logo this can be incorporated into the design of the web page to create a branded look and feel.

E-mail

If potential clients can submit e-mail details on your website you will:

- Gather essential client data

- Acquire new clients

- Increase your potential client-base directly

Retaining and utilising this information will enable you to:

- Send automated e-mails about new products and treatments

221

■ Build stronger client relationships

■ Automatically schedule appointments if a client requires a treatment at periodic intervals

Why the Web Pages You Create Should Be Simple

Easy to update: So that elements can be added and removed from your pages with minimal problems

Easy to use: therefore, the user can navigate the site with clear and defined links. It is sensible to ask a member of your staff to assess the site's functionality and evaluate how user friendly-your website is.

Fast loading 'light' pages: Simple pages download faster, and make an immediate impression on the reader. This is extremely important on the web, where people will leave your site (click off) if your page takes an excessive amount of time to view. Simple pages give a 'clean' look, which often makes a nice visual presentation.

Convey the meaning effectively: You must ensure that visitors to your site will understand what your site is offering them. Visitors will leave your site if they do not understand what service you offer.

Directing traffic to your website

Once your website is designed, tested and launched on the Internet the amount of traffic directed to site can be increased — more traffic, more clients. There are several ways of optimising traffic to your site.

Search engines: Allow people to search for information based on keywords, which they enter into the search engine. The results from a search engine are web pages containing a list of links to web pages with a description of the web page under each link. The links are ordered in relevance to the keywords entered by the person using the search engine, the most relevant at the top, down to the least relevant at the bottom of the list.

Directories: Are another way to direct potential clients. Directories categorise websites into topics and sub-topics. People browse the topics, which contain links to websites related to that topic and a description of that topic.

Sponsored links and adverts: Provide very successful and targeted methods of attracting people to your website. You may have noticed the sponsor links or adverts alongside your search results. These sponsored links are often free to set up and incur no monthly charges. You pay per click no matter how many impressions (number of times your link or advert is displayed). Which means every time a user clicks your link a small charge is incurred. Clicks can cost between 4 pence to over £1, but usually about 8 pence depending on the words or phases. The cost of this can be easily controlled by setting a daily limit on the amount charged. The main benefit with sponsored links is that users who click your link are usually interested in the treatments and products you offer. This is a cost-effective way of advertising and promoting your service.

Web marketing has become the second most important means of attracting new patients into a practice. It makes sense since most individuals find it easier to source information on a variety of subjects via Google or other popular search engines. Unfortunately, large, national medical aesthetic companies dominate Google's first page due to the size of their advertising budget, preventing small independent clinics from capturing their share of new business in their local markets.

Unless small operators can allocate a large amount of financial resources for web optimizing and sponsored links, the chances of an independent clinician outperforming the large national groups is slim. Consequently, small and new businesses cannot access this important source of patient generation.

Beauty Advice Centre – Connecting Clients to Clinician

The Beauty Advice Centre was developed by K-T Training as a knowledge resource for the public. We continuously update the site with information on the medical aesthetic industry. Our long term objective is to make the Beauty Advice Centre the most popular information resource site for the public. Our primary objective for developing the site is to market independent clinicians and small clinics to their local market. Therefore, the site has a locator which allows the public to search for clinicians in their local area. A list of only five clinics for any particular category will appear when the potential client types in their post code into the locator. This means that we will only take five competitive clinics per area. The listed clinics have the flexibility to showcase their clinic on the Beauty Advice Centre by placing clinic photographs and before and after results. The clinic can also attach their website link and other contact information to push the potential client to click onto their site or call the clinic for an appointment.

Independent clinicians can purchase a semi-annual or annual membership to be listed on the site. Eighty percent of the combined membership fee will be allocated to web optimization and sponsored link marketing for the Beauty Advice Centre. For instance, new clients searching for skin clinics in Oxford will most probably go to Google and type in "skin peel oxford". In every instance, a large national clinic's website will appear at the top of the first page of Google. The plan is to use the group's membership fee to optimize the Beauty Advice Centre on page one of Google and at the top of the sponsored link list. Clinicians listed on the site will now have equal opportunity to market their services and compete with the large national groups. Best of all, the site is independent and we endorse all clinicians listed on the site. Listing on the Beauty Advice Centre is a must for new and established clinics. There are limited spaces available so call us for more information on The Beauty Advice Centre. The Beauty Advice Centre web address is www.beautyadvicecentre.co.uk. The site will be promoted extensively through the Beauty Society Magazine and web marketing.

5.2 External Promotions

Information seminars

Information seminars held within your practice or at an outside venue should be part of your promotional strategy. You can advertise the event in the local newspaper and request attendees to reply by a certain date. The attendance should be kept to a maximum of 25 individuals. Everyone likes to get something for free so it might be an idea to mention in the ad that attendees' names will be entered in a draw for a free treatment. You may want to have one of your suppliers sponsor the evening with free products. The event can be an informal wine and cheese evening where the public is invited to attend a free presentation on the entire scope of facial rejuvenation procedures. You may want to conduct a joint presentation with non-competitive businesses that provide other services that are in demand by cosmetic clients. For example, you may want to combine your presentation with a personal trainer, anti-ageing specialists, cosmetic dentist or a well-known make-up artist. However, I prefer seminars that have more focused objectives. Most seminars that I have attended try to cover too much information. It is best to develop a seminar strategy at the beginning of the year. Identify all the areas that are of interest to your target market. In plastic surgery, we know that nose reshaping, liposuction, buttocks lift, upper arm lifts and facelifts are popular procedures. Each seminar should be focused around a few procedures and not the whole scope of plastic surgery. If your advertisements are designed well, you will attract individuals who are interested in the procedures you intend to speak on, and you're more likely to convert these individuals into clients.

Tips on Conducting an Effective Presentation

Delivering your presentations effectively involves using a proven four-step process: Plan, Prepare, Practice and Present. Follow these guidelines and your message will have high impact on your audiences.

The plan: Knowledge of your audience. If your seminar is on facelifts, for example, you know that most of the attendees will be female in the 40–65 age range. Their concerns include the following: downtime, safety, outcome and cost. Make sure the presentation includes answers to these concerns.

Define the purpose of your talk based on the outcome you seek with your audience: In most cases the objective of the presentation will be to:

- Inform
- Persuade
- Motivate to action

225

Do not put together a presentation haphazardly without any objective. The presentation needs to be dynamic enough to move the audience from mere interest in the subject to "I want to have the procedure".

Prepare: It's important to find an attention-grabbing opening. Use a question related to the audience's need. For example, I sometimes begin a presentation by saying to the audience, "do you find that as we age, it gets more difficult to get dressed in the morning, nothing seems to look good any more, and you spend an exorbitant amount of money on miracle night creams, which promise everything and do nothing. That is what we are here to talk about. We are really here to talk to you about an industry that helps its clients to enhance their appearance. Therefore, improving their quality of life. This is the objective of the (..........) Clinic

Pay a sincere compliment: I think that every woman is beautiful in her own way. Plastic surgery can enhance people's lives if we use it not to change ourselves but to enhance what we already have.

Relate a relevant incident: Illustrate and support key points with evidence and visuals. Before and after photographs are essential ingredients to a successful seminar. As is demonstrating the technique — demonstrate a non-invasive procedure if you can. Let the audience evaluate your bedside manner. Talk to the audience about the patient's face. Identify good features. Identify the areas that can be enhanced with the different alternatives available in the practice. You need to educate the audience on the idea that ageing is dynamic and combination of several treatments is needed to create youthfulness including cosmetic dentistry.

In your demonstration, you are not only demonstrating the procedure, you are trying to connect with the audience by demonstrating the following: your technical skills, your communication skills, your interpersonal skills and most importantly, your perceptiveness of what is important to the audience. You want the audience to trust you.

Public Relations

Find out about your local newspapers, TV station and radio station. You might find it really helpful to speak to a local PR agency in your community that has strong contacts with the media. The public is very interested in aesthetic medicine. Fashion journalists should be hungry for news in this area. Approach journalists with the confidence that you are providing information that they need. You do not have to plead with them for space. Point out that you are as interested as they are in providing the public with factual and current information. Inform them you are always available to speak on the subject. Invite them to come and see your facility and observe some simple procedures. Provide a free treatment if possible and educate the journalists on issues that are important in selecting a good surgeon, cosmetic physician or cosmetic dentist.

Designate one or two media contact people in your office – the chances are that you will be seeing patients when the call comes from the press. You may find it helpful to name your office manager or assistant as the contact person who should handle media calls.

If a reporter does contact you, handle the request quickly and efficiently. Find out the five 'W's. Who is calling? What media outlet he or she represents? Where the reporter can be reached. When they phoned and Why? Make sure your staff relays the media request to you immediately. If you can take the call, speak to the reporter to learn more about their request for information.

Keep your message simple. Do not focus too much on yourself but on the issue. Speak about your clients and how they react to the procedures you perform. Be accessible to the reporter. Let the reporter know that she/he is welcome to call back if something needs to be checked.

If you haven't been able to speak to the reporter when he/she phoned, always call back. You may not perform the procedure the journalist is asking about, but you may be able to recommend someone who can. Here is your opportunity to develop a relationship with the reporter.

Personal Appearances on TV Interviews

Appearance: Neutral colours such as navy and black are best. Choose a simple but elegant tie for men. Ladies should wear basic colours — loud clothes will distract from you.

Body Language: Sit comfortably but maintain good posture. Do not move around too much because that can be distracting and annoying to the cameramen. Speak to the interviewer and not the camera, and portray a warm and considerate image.

Your message: Be concise and to the point. Long-winded answers will lose their point.

Your voice: Speak normally — not too slow or fast. It might be wise to practice before you are interviewed. Do not speak in a monotonous manner. Emphasize certain points and use your hands sometimes if you are comfortable doing so. Do not lecture, speak in a conversational tone. Speak in lay terms. Make your point in less than two minutes. You will lose the audience if you take longer than two minutes. Enjoy.

The Interview

Most questions fall into these categories: anticipate what the interviewer will ask.

Loaded Question: Why are cosmetic procedures so expensive? This type of question is based on false premise, ignorance or baiting.

Response: Most cosmetic procedures are not expensive if compared to what the public pays for other services (legal, accounting, etc). Then explain the cost involved in carrying out a surgical procedure. Explain your training and the long-term tangible and intangible benefits to the patient.

The Irrelevant Personal Question: Try to avoid any personal question not relevant to the interview.

Response: That is not really relevant to this interview but I will be glad to discuss this issue with you after the programme.

The Hostile Question: Cosmetic doctors are perpetuating vanity and are only interested in making money at the expense of patient's insecurity.

Response: Do not go on the defensive. Respond by saying that the industry is growing at a rapid rate due to growing patient demand. Patients want medical solutions for improving their appearance. Go on to speak of the ethics committees and the associations involved in policing unethical practice in cosmetic medicine. Finish off by saying that you are very proud of your work and your patients have a better quality of life as a result of whatever procedure they have had with yourself.

The Disparaging Question: A number of patients have died while having cosmetic surgery — are patients taking a risk?

Response: Every surgical procedure involves some risk. The risk is minor if patients select their doctors wisely. Explain what you do to minimise this risk. Explain situations that can result in death. Explain the importance of patients choosing their doctor wisely and selectively.

Advertising

Advertising is without a doubt the most expensive means of generating new business. If you do plan to engage in an advertising campaign, here are nine rules to follow for effective advertising results:

Audience: You must identify whom you want to reach. We divided the market into different segments that include gender and age ranges. Now decide which segment you want to attract.

Message: What characteristics or services distinguish your practice from the competition? Focus on what makes your practice better than others. It could be your expertise in a particular procedure, or maybe you have discovered a unique surgical technique that minimises down-time and is less expensive than what the market is currently paying. Highlight something about your practice that grabs the audience's attention. Your PR Company should help you with this, or if you do not have a PR agent then contact us for help (yasmin@k-tsolutions.com).

Design: Regardless of budget, good design will contribute to your ad being seen. Good photos, fonts and use of colour are helpful. Review top fashion magazines for ideas or employ a design company.

Medium: Choose the proper medium to communicate your message. Depending on which market you want to target, advertise in the appropriate medium.

Placement of your ad: Ask where the best possible location is and request it. Establish a creative tag line: Get your PR Company to develop some creative and original concepts that will attract attention.

Impact: Your advertisement must always be consistent in design and location. The design cannot change. A person will need to see an ad approximately 10 times before they decide to buy or call you.

Assessment: You must have some way of tracking the success of your campaign. You do not only want to track response, you want to evaluate how many calls were transformed into booked consultations.

Evaluation: If you started your advertising in January, you may want to evaluate the success of the campaign by the first quarter.
Evaluate which of your promotional activities are producing the best results. Based on the results, you may want to make modifications to your promotional strategy.

Example of your Promotional Analysis (1st quarter review)

Promotional Analysis	Total Cost of Activity	Enquiries	Booked Consults	Booked procedures	Average Cost /Procedure
Advertising	£5,000	100	25=25%	10=40%	£500
Yellow Pages	£3000	150	30=20%	15=50%	£200
Brochures	£2000	200	50=25%	30=60%	£66.66
Newspaper Ads	£1800	400	100=25%	5=5%	£360.00
Magazines	£1,000	100	80=80%	3=3%	£333.0
Web Optimization	£600	200	30=15%	20=66%	£30.0
Doc Shop	£1000	400	10=02%	10=100%	£100
Pay per click	£1500	270	150=55%	75=50%	£20.00
Newsletters	£1000	50	40= 80%	20=50%	£50
Seminars	£2000	50	50=100%	40=80%	£50
Referral Program	£4000				
Frequent User Program	£1,000				

- You need to analyse all of your promotional activities and determine which ones provide the highest return on your investment.

- Some activities such as web optimization might show a low average cost per procedure but these enquiries take up a lot of your employees' time and resources to move the inquiry into a booked consultation. This must be taken into account.

- The best promotional activities are those that produce high response rate, high consultation booking rate and high-booked procedure rate. (Patient Referrals)

- When you have identified your key activities, spend more resources promoting yourself through these promotional activities.

- Eliminate activities with low ROI.

- For those activities that show a high response/ low consultation ratio, you need to identify if your receptionist is weak in converting difficult calls into booked consultations or if the calls are truly useless. Find out what kind of questions are being asked by the callers and ask the receptionist for his/her views on why clients are not committing to a consultation. If he/she needs training to help him/her respond to questions more efficiently, provide him/her with the necessary training.

"Many a small thing has been made large by the right kind of advertising". Mark Twain

5.3 Business plan

A detailed business plan sets out the objectives of the organisation over a stated period of time - usually 3 to 5 years. The plan should quantify as many of the objectives as possible, providing a monthly cash flow for at least two years. The business must also outline its strategy and the tactics it intends to use to achieve its objectives. The business plan sets out how the owners/managers of a business intend to realise their objectives. Without such a plan a business is likely to drift.

The business plan serves several purposes:

- It enables the practice owner to think through the business in a logical and structured way and to set out the stages in the achievement of the business objectives

- It enables the practice's managers/owners to review progress against the plan

- Ensures that both the resources needed to carry out the strategy and the time when they are required are identified

- Is a means for making all employees aware of the business's direction

- Is an important document when looking for finance

- It links the detailed, short-term, one-year budget to the business plan

I strongly recommend that every cosmetic practice develop a formal document that outlines its long and short term objective. This can be done with the help of your financial manager or with the help of a business consultant. Contact K-T Solutions for business assistance if required. www.k-tsolutions.com or call us at 01793324941

Developing Your Business Plan

In developing your business plan you will be writing a document that is tailor-made for your practice.

There are standard sections that are common to most business plans, which I have not discussed so far.

Mission Statement: Your mission statement is a description of what you want to achieve for your business in the long term. The mission statement might be published in several places (on promotional material, in the board room, waiting-room and definitely in each treatment room) as well as in the business plan.

There is (thankfully) no standard format for a mission statement. However, an effective mission statement should contain the following characteristics:

- Brief: it should be easy to understand and remember

- Flexible: it should be able to accommodate change

- Distinctive: it should make the business stand out

Examples

Sainsbury's plc: Our mission is to be the consumer's first choice for food, delivering products of outstanding quality and great service at a competitive cost through working 'faster, simpler and together'.

Churchill China: To be a leading provider to the tabletop market and deliver value through excellence in design, quality and client service

Make a list of what you want your practice to be. Once you have completed your list, combine all your objectives into one or two sentences. This is your mission statement. Have your mission statement framed and visible to your clients and staff.

Here are two examples of mission statements for medical aesthetics practices.

Example 1

At xyz clinic, we recognise that a person's self image is based on a combination of inner and outer beauty. We take pride in working with each client to develop individualized enhancement programs to help fusion ones inner and outer self resulting in a better quality of life.

Example 2

Mission Statement

The objective of Your Clinic is to become a leading cosmetic clinic that provides non surgical medical aesthetics treatments, extensive range of beauty treatments, anti-ageing therapies, and diet and nutrition services to all ethnicities by partnering with the most innovative specialists in the field, who can deliver excellent treatment results, superior pre and post treatment care and advise, and the most innovative and diverse product offering.

Client Promise

- Excellent treatment results
- Good value
- Superior Client Care
- Educated and informed advisors
- Multiple locations for client convenience
- Multiple finance options to meet the needs of its patients
- Innovative treatments that provide predictable and superior treatment results

Market Situation: This is a general description of the market in which you are working. It will include:

Size of the market: start with your client base and the surrounding area.

Here is a reference source for you to contact if you require information on your local market.

Demographic reports can give an invaluable understanding of the types of people living within a particular area, enabling you to make successful decisions.

The Demographic Overview report contains information on gender, age, marital status, income, health, housing type and tenure, ethnicity and economic activity. At just £49 (+VAT) there is no better way to gain a quick understanding of local populations.

There is a wealth of other demographic data available, so please let us know if you have a specific request and we will try our best to help CAMEO UK is a profiling system which takes demographics a step further. At postcode level it provides a clear understanding of customers in terms of lifestyle and behaviour. Knowing leisure activities, brand preferences, holiday destinations, newspaper readership, etc. can help you predict consumer behaviour and act accordingly.

Call us free on 0800 043 1825 or email us at info@cartogen.co.uk

---

- Description of your client base: age, income, gender, etc. You need to determine if your existing client base will sustain your objectives, or if you need to engage in additional promotions to draw new clients to the practice.
- Is there a need for the services that you are intending to provide in your market? You do not have to conduct a needs assessment, but you need to be realistic about your local market. This is a high end service and sometimes your market may desire the service but cannot afford the cost of the procedures you offer. Most clinicians

tend to choose Muscle Relaxant training as their first course without assessing if the local market can afford the treatment. If you are in a low income market, it might be best to choose less expensive treatments to provide to the local market such as chemical peels, skin care, and mesotherapy.

Procedure Pricing:

■ What is going to be your pricing strategy? Do you plan to undercut your competitor or to sell on service and other value propositions to attract new clients?

What is the most powerful media in your market?:
e.g. radio, newspaper, etc.

Competitors:

■ List your competitors

■ Identify your competitors' strengths and weaknesses.

■ How will you compete against your main competitor?

■ Do you see any future competitors?

Please list the Strengths, Weaknesses, Opportunities and Threats of each of your main competitors. This is known as a SWOT analysis and provides a clear overview of the situation.

Issues to consider include: length of experience in business, how they market themselves (e.g. innovative, healthy, natural, the products/sectors they specialise in; the client types they specialise in, their key people (e.g. the skills they have that offer the company an advantage) pricing structure (are they more or less expensive than you) estimated revenues, growth constraints, and most significant factors in their success.

Ask someone, e.g. an employee, to book a consultation with each competitor. Assess the strengths, weakness and possible threats of each competitor. Below is an example to follow.

Competitive Landscape

Competitive Analysis

FACTOR	Me	Strength	Weakness	Joe Blog	Multi Nationals
Products	Complete offering	★		Same	Same
Price	Value	★		Premium	Premium
Quality	High	★		Medium	High
Selection	Core products	★		Offers everything	Offers everything
Service	Be honest	★			
Reliability	Be honest	★			
Stability	Low if new practice			Established	Established
Expertise	High	★		Low	Low
Company reputation	Low if new	★			
Location	City centre				
Appearance	High	★			
Credit policies					
Advertising	High	★			
Image	Superior	★			
Staff	Well Trained	★			

237

Environment: Economically is your market in a position to seek the benefits of your products?

If your practice is in a low-income area, then it is probably unrealistic to set very high financial goals for the aesthetic component of the business.

Local long term strategies and objectives: Where do you want your business to go over the next 3–5 years, and how are you going to get there? List the objectives you want to set for yourself in this period to bring about the desired result.

Please consider financial as well as non-financial objectives. For example, include the financial goals that were discussed in the previous section. In each chapter I make recommendations on both financial and non-financial issues.

Short- term objectives: What are the current year's business objectives? What do you intend doing over the next calendar year to achieve your long-term objectives? This information was discussed in Chapter one.

Activities: What do you need to do in order to reach your short-term objectives? How do you plan on implementing these tasks to achieve your objectives? What kind of support do you need from your staff or from outside consultants to achieve your goals? Discussed throughout the book and needs to be outlined in the business plan.

Budget for next year: Estimate sales and cost of doing business for the next year. This subject is covered in Chapter 1 in the financial planning section and the procedure pricing section.

 This book provides you with 85% of answers to complete your business plan. Local demographic study and competitive analysis information will have to be completed by you. The importance of the business plan is for your benefit. By completing this document, you will have a good idea if your business strategy will succeed. The business plan should be done before the business begins to minimize financial risks.

Once you have completed your business plan and have identified your long and short term objectives, you need to develop a marketing plan which will support the financial objectives laid out in the business plan.

Marketing Activities

How do I guarantee marketing success? Marketing is not a precise science and the opportunity for failure is great. People often get carried away with an initiative and do not focus on the specific issues that will determine success or failure.

The pre-marketing checklist

The pre-marketing checklist is designed to maximise the benefits from your marketing initiatives. It will focus your time and the time of your support staff and will optimise marketing expenditure.

What are your exact objectives-what are you trying to achieve? Increase sales, raise product awareness, educate or influence?

Who are you targeting? Current clients, new clients or people who can influence clients? The more focused the audience the greater your success. If you try to be 'all things to all individuals', you will fail!

What is your budget? Are you using the budget effectively? Are you getting a return on your marketing investment? Could this money be better used elsewhere? For example, most practices do not utilise the power of the Internet. Most cosmetic clients use the Internet to search for information. Would it not be more efficient and less expensive to use the Internet as a major source of advertising?

Who are your competitors and how are you different? Compare your business and products to your competitors.

What is your message? What are you trying to get across? The more focused your message, the greater the impact. You need to be different!

Are you demonstrating your expertise? Are you adding value? Are you providing something different in your marketing message? If you are not demonstrating your expertise or adding value to your clients you should consider another initiative.

Can you measure the effectiveness? Ideally, this should be in terms of sales, but also word of mouth (WOM), press coverage, enquiries etc, all of which can be tracked.

Is this initiative part of an ongoing campaign? All too often one-off initiatives are a waste of time! Each initiative must be followed up on an on-going basis.

Your business is driven and revolves around the relationship with your clients. 'Relationship based' marketing is different from 'consumer marketing'. The objectives of any 'relationship based' marketing campaign should be:

To move as quickly as possible from mass communication with a wide audience to face-to-face selling opportunities. High involvement products such as aesthetic medicine need high contact to achieve ongoing sales and to develop relationships.

Focus! The broader the audience you attempt to reach, the weaker the impact. If different clients have different requirements and motivations, one message to all will not be as effective as a targeted message. For example, if you plan to target a young age group, you need to target the message to their specific needs.

One may succeed without a plan but a well laid out plan will get you to your destination quicker. There is something magical about planning and forecasting. You will achieve the results. Without knowing what you want to achieve and how you intend to achieve your goals, you are lost.

The information provided in chapters 1 to 5 will be the meat of your business and your marketing plan. So far, you have answers to the following:

■ Procedure Offering

■ Procedure pricing

- Target Marketing
- Competitive analysis
- Opportunities and risks
- Resource Management
- Bonus plan to motivate employees
- Systems to improve communication with your clients
- Focused promotional plan for your target markets
- Segmenting your market and identifying key procedures for each segment
- Metrics established to measure staff efficiencies
- Mission statement

Summary

My hope is that **Simple Steps to Building Successful Cosmetic Practices** will help its readers to see that relationship marketing and strategic planning is a structured and methodical approach to developing and managing a medical aesthetic business for long-term success and profitability. Clearly, relationship marketing is not about advertising and promotion. It is a much more involved discipline that looks at the whole scope of your practice. It is a structured and methodical approach to creating and keeping clients. The whole discipline revolves around the concept of providing better value for the client, and I am sure this outcome is what most clinic owners want. The better skilled you are at relationship marketing, the more difficult it will be for large or small competitors to threaten your ongoing success.

I would like to conclude this chapter as a workshop in the sense that it leads you through a series of questions that will help you to assess the present position of your practice.

- Do you know where the practice is trying to get to in the long term?
- Have you analysed and segmented your market?
- Do you know your competitive advantage in each segment?
- If so, what is it that you do differently from your competitors?

241

■ Do you know your competitors?

■ Do you provide the best quality of service to your clients?

■ Have you set financial objectives for each business unit?

■ Do you know which segment of the aesthetic market contributes the greatest amount of revenue to your practice?

■ If so, what is your strategy to keep these clients coming back?

■ Do you know what percentage of your client base are repeat clients?

■ Do you have an orientation program for new employees?

■ Is your staff trained in customer service?

■ Do you motivate your employees to meet the practice's objectives?

■ Do you have an in-house training program for your employees?

■ Have you established an incentive scheme for your employees?

■ Do you conduct performance review at the end of each fiscal year?

■ Do you hold regular meetings with your staff to review the performance of the business?

If you answered 'no' to any of these questions, I suggest you roll up your sleeves and get to work. I can guarantee you that if you apply the recommendations given throughout this book; you will not need luck to achieve your goals. You will stand out from the crowd and achieve market dominance. If you require further assistance, please review the services provided by K-T Group. The services offered by each division support the concepts detailed in the book. If you find it difficult to create or execute any of our recommendations contact the company at info@kttraining.co.uk for assistance.

K – T Groups of Companies

■ K-T Training (Procedure Training)

■ K-T Solutions (Consulting Services)

■ Beauty Advice Centre (Web Marketing)

■ K-T Retail Division (Training and Promotional Resources)

■ K-T Business Division (Business Training)

Practice Development Notes

Practice Development Notes

Practice Development Notes

MERZ AESTHETICS

First-rate skin ... by any measure.

Your patients want to know exactly what to expect from aesthetic treatment. Now you have a scientific way to show them.

Introducing the Merz Scales, the first-standardized and validated tool for measuring the skin's aging process. Developed by leading physicians, the Merz Scales give you an objective way to measure your patients' age-related skin changes and talk to them about their treatment options.

To find out more about the Merz Scales and Practitioner Participation Programs contact Merz on 020 8236 3550

Design and Marketing solutions

*On screen media *Web development *Design *Marketing *Logos and branding

Find out how we could help you...

Whether you're looking for a flyer, leaflet, brochure, website, one-off marketing campaign, the full creation of a brand or even a re-design, then lush can tailor a package to suit your budget. For successful design, marketing and production, call lush today!

design: **+44 (0)7525 655305** marketing: **+44 (0)7973 966995**

www.lushdesign.biz

lush* 31-33 Amersham Hill • High Wycombe • Bucks • HP136NU

Lightning Source UK Ltd.
Milton Keynes UK
UKOW06f1528160415

249767UK00001B/6/P